T0198763

# Kindling the Flame

*Reflections on Ritual, Faith, and Family*

## ROBERTA ISRAELOFF

SIMON & SCHUSTER

SIMON & SCHUSTER
Rockefeller Center
1230 Avenue of the Americas
New York, NY 10020
Copyright © 1998 by Roberta Israeloff

SIMON & SCHUSTER and colophon are
registered trademarks of Simon & Schuster Inc.

*Designed by Ruth Lee*

Manufactured in the United States of America

1   3   5   7   9   10   8   6   4   2

Library of Congress Cataloging-in-Publication Data

Israeloff, Roberta, date.
Kindling the flame : reflections on ritual, faith, and family / Roberta Israeloff
p.      cm.
1. Israeloff, Roberta, date—Religion. 2. Jewish women—United States—
Religious life. 3. Judaism—United States. 4. Jews—United States—
Social life and customs. I. Title.
BM726.I87  1998
296.7'15'092—dc21       98-9596
[B]                      CIP

ISBN: 978-1-5011-2751-9

The author gratefully acknowledges permission to reprint the following
previously published material:

"Song ["Now let us honor with violin and flute"]," copyright 1948 by
May Sarton, from *Selected Poems of May Sarton* by Serena Sue Hilsinger
and Lois Brynes, editors. Reprinted by permission of W. W. Norton &
Company, Inc.

"The Far Field," copyright © 1962 by Beatrice Roethke, Administrix
for the Estate of Theodore Roethke, from *The Collected Poems of Theodore
Roethke* by Theodore Roethke. Used by permission of Doubleday, a division of Bantam Doubleday Dell Publishing Group, Inc.

# Acknowledgments

'd like to thank Pam Abrams, Alice Alexiou, Diane Cole, Mary Beth Denniston, Wallace Kaufman, Vicki Lens, Joan Leonard, Eileen Morrone, Joan Reminick, Carol Rubin, Dena Salmon, Elly Silberman, Nancy Wackstein, Judy Weingarten, Celeste Wenzel, and Elizabeth Wix for the inestimable gift of their friendship and wisdom as it guided me writing this book;

Ellen Ostrow, because our thirty-three-year conversation informs its every page;

Becky Saletan, who believed in it from the first, and whose inventiveness and insight rescued it many times;

Denise Roy, for her steadfastness, patience, careful attention, and unflagging encouragement when these qualities were most needed;

Sona Vogel, for helping me to say what I meant to;

Lynn Seligman, on whose clarifying advice and judgment I have come to wholeheartedly depend;

and my family—David, Ben and Jake; Marvin and Phyllis Fleisher; Rae Israeloff; Marcia Israeloff; and Laura Botnaro. They know why.

*In memory of my father,*
*Jack Israeloff;*

*and my grandmothers,*
*Ella Salkoff Engelberg and*
*Fannie Schoendorf Israeloff;*

*and for my mother, Rae Israeloff*

The higher goal of spiritual living is not to amass a wealth of information, but to face sacred moments.

—ABRAHAM JOSHUA HESCHEL
*The Sabbath*

# Contents

# Contents

# CHAPTER 1

# *Time/Place*

 *ueens: Winter 1958*

In the middle of giving me a piano lesson, my grandmother's eyes grew gray and dreamy. "In the winter," she said, "it would freeze over entirely and we'd skate all the way across."

We were in the bedroom I shared with my younger sister. Steam rattled through the radiators; the inside surfaces of the paned windows were runny with condensation. We lived high enough in our apartment building to have a panoramic view of the development parking lot, the park and playground, 73rd Avenue, which we couldn't cross by ourselves, and beyond that the streets of private houses. No one we knew lived there. It was another world.

"What froze?" I asked. An image of Hans Brinker and Holland rose to mind, though I knew very well that wasn't where she'd come from.

"The Baltic. The Baltic Sea. Riga, Latvia," she said, place names coming reluctantly. Usually, when she wanted to refer to the place of her birth and girlhood she said simply "Europe"—not a country, but a continent, one of many continents to which the Jews were dispersed and temporarily put up tents, there being only one enduring country, more of the mind than soil, a country you cart around with you, the portable nation of Israel.

The piano on which I was learning the C scale was a toy; a miniature white baby grand, it rested on the top of my dresser. We stood in front of it, my grandmother and I, while my mother and sister rattled pots and dishes in the kitchen, preparing dinner. The lower part of my grandmother's hand was pudgy, fleshy, but her fingers were bony, her nails grooved, long, and gray. Daintily, she arched her fingers in the air above the tiny plastic keys, placing her thumb on middle C, her pointer on D, her middle finger on E. Then, in an astonishing feat of legerdemain, her thumb disappeared into the cup of her hand and landed on F. Now, magically, she had enough fingers to finish playing the rest of the scale. She didn't close her eyes as she played, just as she didn't when recounting the afternoons she spent ice skating on the Baltic

Sea, yet her eyes changed, as if she were no longer looking out but inward; as if the interior scene were infinitely richer than any she could put into words, every remembrance summoning up so many sounds and smells that the ones wafting in from the kitchen were the palest comparison. She looked this way when she lit candles—every Friday night, to usher in Shabbos, and especially those times during the year when she lit a special candle lodged in a glass in memory of her dead husband. It burned all day and all night.

When she wasn't visiting with our family, she lived alone, a widow, in a two-room apartment in the Bronx. Her greatest daily pleasure was walking down to Jerome Avenue, where she sat with her friends, their pocketbooks placed on their laps like personal, miniature tea tables, their furious conversation—all in throat-clogging Yiddish; not until I studied German in college did I realize how little English my grandmother actually knew—never pausing, not even when the clattering el passed overhead or when they moved from bench to bench, chasing the dwindling afternoon sun. She also loved to sing, throaty, guttural, wordless songs that originated less in her throat and vocal cords than in her chest, from an organ that vibrated as she breathed. As a young girl she had had music lessons and ice-skating lessons. She'd left home when she was fourteen with her older brother, who was escaping conscription into the Russian army. Sometimes he carried her on his back through the snow. Somehow they reached America—not in steerage—where she met a man she'd known from Riga and married him; she had three children and owned a grocery store. She never knew her birthday.

"These things they didn't write down in those days for girls," she told me with an embarrassed laugh, as if the omission were somehow her fault. The brother she came to America with knew his birthday. He became a Zionist, a soldier in Palestine, a dentist, and the patriarch of my grandmother's large, transplanted family—six brothers and sisters, all married, a slew of cousins, most of whom I didn't know.

I had turned eight on my last birthday. The lamp on my dresser was on though it was barely five in the afternoon. Dark already. We had to dress by lamplight in the early morning, too, getting ready for school. Even by noon, when my friends and I walked home for lunch, past the tree whose roots distended the sidewalk, the day looked tired, closer to night than morning.

Some mornings when my sister and I woke up, our window was sheathed in thick, scored, erose ice. If you touched it, the ice melted clear through to the glass, heat from our fingers radiating outward like tiny suns. My sister and I loved to dot the ice with holes and to write our names in the condensation; the frigid glass anesthetized our fingers and made me think of the frozen sea on which my grandmother skated. "Don't do that," my grandmother admonished, wincing from our immodesty, our eagerness to show off, to trumpet our existence, afraid that our script would prove indelible— though of course it disappeared a moment later, a thin layer of soot on our fingertips all that remained.

## East Northport: Fall 1989

Benjamin, my oldest son, was eight; Jacob was three. Sarah and Rachel are the names I would have chosen if I'd had girls. Leah, Samuel, Isaac, Eli, and Rebecca are the names of my friends' children. We recite their names almost apologetically, as if to say, I have no idea where this came from, this inspiration to return to the Bible. Search me.

Ben, beginning second grade, asked if he could take piano lessons. It was also time, I knew, to begin him on the course of study that would culminate in his Bar Mitzvah. I'd known this for a year, yet I did little more than think about it.

"I wish it could just happen," my friends and I told each other whenever we had the luxury of time for a conversation. We all had Hebrew school or Sunday school on the brain, and we all wished the same thing—that our children could receive a religious education with no effort on our part.

In the past, religion had unfailingly surfaced, unbidden, like a thin but persistent underground spring, for milestone events. I married a man who was Jewish; in fact, I never seriously dated anyone who wasn't. When my parents asked me if I intended to be married by a rabbi, bracing themselves for my objection, I said sure. When they asked, after the birth of each of my sons, if I was planning on having a *brith,* a ritual circumcision, I said of course. These were less conscious decisions than simple accessions. I said yes almost reflexively, leaving them to nail down the details, which, in their relief, they were more than happy to do—asking their rabbi to officiate, seeing to his fee, inviting guests, hiring caterers. All I did was show up.

If only I could simply show up for my son's Bar Mitzvah. If only we could have the ceremony without having to join or attend a synagogue. If only my parents could once again be in charge. But that was out of the question. First of all, my father was dead, and my mother had neither the energy nor the emotional resources to shoulder the responsibility by herself. This was solidly my event to plan and produce; I couldn't palm it off on anyone else. Joining a synagogue was the first step.

Yet for me to pursue synagogue membership seemed the height of hypocrisy. My sense of God, of spirituality, never jibed with anything I'd heard in any synagogue or from any rabbi. My most spiritual moments were intensely private—hiking up a mountain, listening to a Beethoven string quartet, sitting on my bed or in my study with a book of Emily Dickinson's poems, Shakespeare's sonnets, the writings of Lao-tse. I resented organized religion philosophically. Praying at preordained times—Friday nights or Saturday mornings—struck me as not only ridiculous, but antithetical to human nature.

For rabbis, those posturing men full of platitudes, I had no use at all. I'd never forgiven the one who officiated at my grandmother's funeral, when I was twenty, who throughout the eulogy called her by an incorrect first name and mangled her second. How could anyone be comforted by such a man? But the worst was yet to come. After the service, he stationed himself outside the chapel door to offer personal condolences to the family, stringing together a litany of clichés he'd relied on one too many times, for all that came out that particular morning, as he clasped my shoulder and looked deep into my eyes, was a hapless, pathetic string of nonsense syllables and meaningless babble.

## Syosset: Spring 1964

"So you want to send your daughter to Hebrew school," said the rabbi, fixing his thin, penetrating gaze first on my sister, then on my parents. In his sleek, navy blue suit and rep tie, sporting a pencil-thin mustache, he looked more lawyer than scholar.

Only minutes, it seemed, had elapsed between the move from our Queens apartment to a suburban ranch house on Long Island and this appointment with the rabbi of the local Jewish center in his book-lined, paneled study. My father had arranged it—my father, who, until this moment, had barely been able to contain his disdain for anything having to do with religion. When his mother would gather us close to her while she lit Sabbath candles, I could see his eyes dart around the room in a desperate effort to escape, as if she were kissing him on the lips rather than asking him to witness her prayers. Though he'd been bar mitzvahed, I'd never seen him do one religious act; he ceded candle lighting, prayers, and attendance at services to the women in his life.

"May I ask you, what about your older daughter? Did she attend religious school?" The rabbi addressed my parents, though I was sitting directly in front of him.

"I'm afraid I made a terrible mistake," my mother said, explaining how, until now, she'd refrained from joining a synagogue—the Orthodox shul in our old neighborhood reminding her too much of the shtetl, the Reform too watered-down, the Conservative too far away to walk to on the holidays. "It's my biggest regret," my mother concluded. "And now it's too late."

The rabbi didn't disagree but nodded sympathetically. I didn't regret anything. I knew about being Jewish, and I'd learned it from the horse's mouth, my grandmother, the most otherworldly person I could imagine. Together we'd sounded out melodies on the piano, and sat on the foldout couch that was her bed, reading Bible stories from a glossy picture book with a huge, bearded, beneficent Moses clutching the Ten Commandments on the cover.

From watching her, I knew that Jewish holidays fell at odd times, in the middle of the week, at different times of the year, sometimes in one month, sometimes in another, Jewish time running not in counterpoint, but in opposition to the school calendar, a capricious, elfin syncopation, an irrepressible wildness that seemed to delight in confounding. Holidays when we didn't go to school, eat, write, ride in the car, began not in the morning, but the night before. You welcomed them by lighting candles that brought the dying outer light indoors. Being Jewish was waking up at night and seeing the house slightly illuminated but so subtly that you had to rub your eyes to make sure; you could see it best when you looked at it like starlight, not directly but askance.

"It's not enough," the rabbi admonished, putting his fingertips down on his desk and rising slightly, as if inviting levitation, "to send a child to Hebrew school; you all need to become involved in Jewish life." The implicit threat in his voice chilled us, turned everything I knew to be fluid about my religion into stone. Clearly he didn't expect to see much of our family again. But my father was not one to countenance a charge of hypocrisy.

Within days he announced that we would begin attending services on Friday nights—even though this decision meant that my mother had to work double time to get dinner on the table, clean up, and propel us all out of the house, even though my junior high school sponsored a social on Fridays. While my friends primped in front of the mirror and sifted through their closets for the perfect outfit, I drove with my family to synagogue. While my friends swayed to the music and waited for boys to ask them to dance, I stared at the prayer book, unable to read a word of Hebrew. I read the English, wondering if the original had more fervor than the tepid translation. Why why why was I here? I'd cry to myself during services, during which time itself seemed suspended. Of what value was it? The same songs, the same prayers, the same instructions, week after excruciating week: "Please rise, please be seated, read responsively in English, read in Hebrew." The only part I could stomach were the songs. Not knowing the Hebrew, I sang wordlessly, as my grandmother had.

"The Sabbath is a beautiful bride," the rabbi intoned. *"L'cho dodie."* At this very moment, my friends were crowding around the tiny mirror in the steamy girls' bathroom, shrieking over the boy's ID bracelet one of them had received or crying over the one another had to relinquish. "All week we wait for the Sabbath to come, for the rest and beauty of the Sabbath."

What the rabbi called rest and beauty I knew to be something else entirely. From my grandmother I'd also learned that Shabbos and all the holidays were days of shall nots, of denial, of self-abnegation. There was an entire universe of activity in which she wouldn't partake at those times—simply would not. Wouldn't take the subway or go in a car. Wouldn't cook. Wouldn't write a word or turn on the television or use the telephone even though she was all alone. Wouldn't spend the holidays with us. Would not.

Don't write, don't run, don't eat that, don't eat too much, don't move around, don't even think about it—this was Judaism's heart of negation around which my grandmother had constructed her life. But of all the injunctions, none was stronger than Don't ask.

I wish now that I'd mustered the courage to call her bluff, to ask her what was in that oversize valise of her past that she carried around with her, and to persist even after she replied, with a sly smile, "And what valise is that?" Had she lived in a wooden house? Was it in the city or in the country? How many rooms did it have? What did she eat at her meals? What did her father do for a living? What was he like, my grandfather—a man I'd never known, but for whom I'd been named? Yet her stubbornness defeated me. As a child I couldn't even articulate these questions. There was something in my grandmother's gray stoutness that stopped my tongue: not only didn't she encourage questions, but she seemed to repel them, to render me incapable of asking them. For many years I assumed that her husband's premature death pained her beyond words, but now I think her muteness stemmed more from the stark boldness of her emigration, her break with her parents, her country, her history. "Don't ask," she said to me in a million wordless ways, the past a multitentacled beast whose body contains a sadness too great to comprehend.

I accepted her silence without understanding it. For me the past had only two compartments: in the first I stored those rich, vibrant memories I could personally recall; and into the second I dumped everything else. In this deeper past, time had but one dimension, so that World War II, which ended only seven years before I was born, was tinged with the same historical remoteness as Bible stories.

The very notion that the past could be a minefield of pain, that people would want to suppress rather than evoke and examine their memories, was completely foreign to my friends and me growing up during the affluent 1960s. "Don't ask; don't even think about it"—this was the last credo by which I wanted to live. I yearned to question everything, to be ashamed of nothing. Being Jewish seemed to work against everything vital in my life, against every natural thought and urge I had.

"I'm not going to Friday night services anymore," I told my father the week I began ninth grade. "It means nothing to me. I hate it. You go, but leave me home." His eyes darted around the room; I knew he was formulating a response. But in the end he left without saying a word.

## Long Island: Winter 1985

In the backseat of the real estate agent's immaculate gray Mercedes, I nibbled crackers, apple slices, raisins, and nuts from a paper bag. Next to me, Ben played with an action figure, moving it on the door handle and up the window, director of his own private movie. David sat up front, asking question after question about the town's tax rates, percentage of high school students who attend Ivy League schools, proximity to garbage dumps.

The driver, a hyper-groomed young man who couldn't possibly have children, glanced at me in his rearview mirror. "She never stops eating, does she?" he asked David. Then to me, "You eat as if you're expecting twins," he said.

"I am," I said, and that shut him up. And lucky for you, I

added to myself, for if I weren't, we wouldn't be here. We'd be in our snug Upper West Side apartment, figuring out where to place a crib. But even I had to admit that two cribs would never fit, no matter how much furniture we moved.

Up and down the deserted suburban streets we drove, house hunting, as my father used to call it. He and my mother had shopped for the perfect house for about eight long years—as long as the Jews had wandered in the desert, it seemed to my sister and me—and we'd just about resigned ourselves to staying in our Queens apartment when one Saturday afternoon they walked into a modest but spacious ranch on a quiet, tidy street and said, "This is it. We'll take it." Their one impulsive act.

I had yet to experience that feeling. Dutifully I followed David, trooping into house after house, asking indelicate questions, peering into intimate places like medicine cabinets, the backs of closets, corners of basements, studying the frightened eyes of people in the midst of upheaval and wondering, Could I live here? Sometimes I thought it would be easier for me to imagine moving if they'd just leave their furniture. I'd easily leave mine behind for the people who moved into our apartment.

It struck me, as we wove in and out of neighborhoods, that though David and I considered ourselves such mavericks to even consider moving out of New York City, we were actually riding a ripple set in motion eighty years earlier. If the Lower East Side is ground zero of American Judaism, where our great-grandparents found cold-water flats and set about scratching out a living, then each successive generation has moved steadfastly north and east, by steps, first to Brooklyn or the bucolic Bronx, then Queens, Nassau, and now Suffolk County. Each address was a crest in a wave emanating from the epicenter, losing energy as it traveled farther from its source.

Yet each of these distances was microscopic compared to my grandmother's giant step from Riga to America. How had she done it? How did any immigrant do it? I couldn't stand the thought of moving forty miles away from everything I found familiar. I felt like crying, the way my grandmother had when my mother announced that she wanted to move from the Bronx to Queens. "So far away!" she'd pouted, as if we were moving to the ends of the earth—the way she herself had done.

To visit us in Queens she had to take two subways and a bus. She arrived on Tuesdays and left on Friday morning, so she'd get home in time for Shabbos. At least there was an Orthodox shul nearby, which she could attend in a pinch; at least there were Jewish bakeries and parks with benches where she could sit in the sun—though she missed her bench and her friends, their faces trained upon the last traces of Bronx sunlight filtering through the metallic filigree of the relentless el—and strike up a conversation in Yiddish with another grandmother, marveling at these green patches of Queens, at their healthy American grandchildren who tore through the playground on their bikes, jumped from the swings, climbed backward up the sliding pond, like *vilde cheye,* wild beasts.

But ten years later, when my mother informed her that she was buying a house in Nassau County—that was another story. Now her unhappiness with our move turned spiteful. "You call him a rabbi?" she asked after attending Friday night services. "He looks like a banker." She hated the synagogue: it was too brightly lit, everyone was too dressed up, men and women sat together. And in our house she couldn't find a comfortable chair. "How can you live here?" she demanded of my mother from her post at the window, peering through the venetian blinds at the deserted, well-kept streets and lawns. "Here where no one walks? Here with all the goyim?"

God, how I'd hated that word. It made me shudder, made me feel dead inside, as if she had said "nigger." In it was consolidated all my distaste for Yiddish and more. "It simply means 'non-Jew,' " my parents and grandparents said, feigning innocence, when I asked them please, *please* don't use that word. Of course it meant mouthfuls more: it was full of suspicion, distrust, superiority all rolled into one slight word. Us and them.

And my grandmother's assessment of the population wasn't nearly accurate. Many of my friends were Jewish—not that it mattered to me then, or that I thought about it for one second. But to argue with her was useless. Anything outside of the Bronx was incurably *trayf,* nonkosher.

"Are there any synagogues in this community?" I asked, interrupting the real estate agent's colloquy. My question surprised me. Though I'd lived in Manhattan for ten years, I had no idea where a single synagogue was located; in fact, I couldn't recall the last time I'd set foot in one.

But it was clear to me, house hunting from the backseat of the real estate agent's car, that neighborhoods had a certain flavor or cast to them, which made them more or less appealing to me. It was a question of *tam*—that was it, the perfect word, a Yiddish word I hadn't used in my entire life, though I'd heard it plenty of times. Loosely translated, it means "taste" or "flavor," radiating outward to indicate a feeling of similarity, of consonance. But like all good Yiddish words, it starts inextricably in the mouth, in the taste of food, in the senses.

## East Northport: Winter 1989

"Why are we the only house on the block without Christmas lights?" my son asked me. In truth, three other houses remained lightless, but it seemed too slight a number to quibble over. I knew what he meant.

He was referring to a faint unease, a sense of not belonging, despite the fact that the community to which we had finally moved, though only a quarter Jewish, supported three synagogues. I felt it, too, at the school bus stop where I waited with other moms for the kids to get home, when every morning and afternoon conversation concerned holiday preparations. And in the butcher, and the five-and-dime store, where the clerks routinely handed me my change and said, "Have a Merry Christmas." As if it hadn't ever occurred to them that all of their customers might not celebrate Christmas. As if in December everyone's Christian, just as on St. Patrick's Day everyone's Irish.

Yet I sensed a certain bellicosity on those few occasions when I responded, "But I don't celebrate Christmas." As if I weren't being a good sport. As if I were ruining everyone's good clean fun. I took to simply saying, "Same to you," and wondering why I never felt this way when I lived in Manhattan—or, for that matter, when I was growing up in Nassau County. Was that neighborhood more Jewish? Had times changed? Had I?

Why, at the PTA meeting I'd recently attended, did I feel so alone? Why couldn't I shake the feeling that I was an outsider? Why did the sight of the trimmed Christmas tree in the lobby dismay me so? The conversations I tried to get rolling fell flat. People would stop talking before I thought they would; I'd start talking before they were finished. When I explained, to a woman who asked, the significance of the dreidel game—that it was a way for Jews to defy the edict not to study—and she commented, "Isn't that crafty?" I said nothing. I didn't call her attention to the fact that she was promulgating an ancient anti-Semitic stereotype. Apparently I'd lived nearly forty years of my life in America without realizing that I was a member of a minority.

Perfunctorily I began scouting synagogues. Though all of the synagogues within my town were within convenient carpooling distance of my home, all were equally out of the question: the Orthodox too rigid and misogynist; the Reform too self-conscious and glitzy, every pew and light switch affixed with a plaque identifying the donor; the Conservative too stodgy, full of everything I'd grown up with—sisterhood, Hadassah, men's clubs, United Jewish Appeal fund-raisers, an attempt to forge a compromise between the Reform and Orthodox that in the end suited no one. There I was, surrounded by a veritable smorgasbord of contemporary Judaism, none of it remotely appetizing. It was beginning to sound like the old joke about the shipwrecked Jew, alone on a deserted island, who, when asked why he built two shuls, points to one and says, "That one I don't go to."

Had my father agonized over which synagogue to join? I didn't recall that he had. He naturally gravitated to the Conservative synagogue, which was devoted to conserving the traditions of the past but with a little less rigidity than the Orthodox. His neighbors and co-workers attended this synagogue. That was good enough for him.

What had propelled him to join? I'd always assumed the obvious: that he wished to redress a wrong, to give his younger daughter the religious education of which he'd inadvertently deprived me. But maybe that wasn't it. Maybe there was more to it. Days after his death, I'd begun compiling a list of questions I wished I could ask him, some as trivial as where he'd put a piece of cross-stitching I'd asked him to frame. I longed to add this one: not simply why he had joined a synagogue, but why with such urgency; and why, for the remaining course of his life, the religion he'd abandoned as a child and young man became so important to him.

For not only did he join a synagogue, but he became an active member, insinuated himself into its very core. One by one, first I, then my sister, then my mother, all defected from Friday night services. But my father's resolve redoubled in the face of our abandonment. Resolutely he began attending not only Friday night services, but Saturday morning as well.

Then he signed up for adult education courses, took on the chairs of various committees, did everything, it seemed, but run for president.

His involvement became such a big part of his life, of who he was, that I actually thought, on the evening I learned that the troubling symptoms he'd been experiencing of late were manifestations of bladder cancer, He can't have cancer. He's too pious.

My last visit with him, as it turned out, was on a Saturday morning. I walked into my parents' bedroom—my father rested on a hospital bed adjacent to the double bed he and my mother had shared for nearly forty years—and found the Sabbath prayer book opened facedown on his stomach.

"Is this a comfort to you?" I asked, indicating the book.

He shrugged, just barely, and made a motion with his hand—take it away. I put a bookmark in the book and placed it within his reach, knowing full well that he was too weak to pick it up himself.

"Have you made peace?" I asked him—words I could hardly believe I was uttering. "Say what you have to say," my husband had warned me ominously. He'd lost a sister; he knew, as I didn't, about what couldn't be said. And this, I realized, was what I most needed to know.

"Yes," he said, reaching for my hand. "I have. You've been wonderful children." He spoke so haltingly, it was excruciating. "I only wish I had a little more time. To see Ben's Bar Mitzvah."

I had plenty of time to think through this penultimate conversation—the contradiction it posed. Had he made peace with the fact of his dying if he still wanted more time? And why the Bar Mitzvah? Nine years sounded almost greedy. And if he made it to that, wouldn't he want more?

He already knew that though the twin pregnancy had miscarried, we still intended to have another child and that he would be the namesake for this baby. I wanted to say many more things, but I noticed that my father wasn't listening. He'd slipped beyond the silver cords that tied him to his family, cords he himself wove, within which he had always found comfort and unabashed happiness. He retreated into himself, as self-contained, as remote, as unreachable, as a newborn baby. He looked like a newborn; in fact, he reminded me of my firstborn, Benjamin, with his black hair and dark eyes, though Ben had looked older at birth than my father in death.

I sat with my father for a while, thinking that having children had anchored me to the physical world, and to time, in ways I hadn't before experienced. For the first year of Ben's life I paid attention to the changing seasons in ways I never had. Winter was difficult because the baby had to be dressed in so many clothes; you had to mount a campaign against the weather just to go outside, to keep him warm and dry, to keep from slipping on ice. Spring was full of promise because you could spend long days outside at the playground and sandbox. Summer brought true easy living—endless days, languorous nights. Ben brought weather into my life just as my father brought news of the rhythms of birth and death.

We talk about biological clocks ticking away when we want to conceive, but my clock started the moment Ben was born. For months I'd been expecting, dreaming of, a red-haired girl. Lying on my back, hoarse from the exertions of labor, I kept yelling, "Is it a boy or a girl?," the bullet of life inside me pushing its way out as if already late for several appointments. And my husband, sounding more amazed than I'd ever heard him, said, "It's a boy," just as the doctor caught him, cradled him—my son—so I could see him draw his first breath, study his well-formed genitals, his dark hair, his pharaonic profile. A boy. A Jewish boy—replete with a long line of ancestors behind him and progeny ahead of him: my fulcrum of creation.

There he was, at the beginning of his life, in the doctor's arms, dripping with blood and the secretions of my body that had nourished and lubricated him, there he was exposed to the age-inducing air, the world in which he'd grow old and eventually die—there he was. I fell back on the pillows, grateful beyond words that labor was over, that I'd met my biological imperative; I'd reproduced myself on earth, repli-cated my genetic material. Hungrily I reached for him, to hold him, to put him to my breast, to touch him, watch him suck up all the vitality in the room. I was already forgotten, leftovers, yesterday's news.

"Parents are reluctant to make arrangements for their child's Bar Mitzvah," I once heard a rabbi say, "because they are forced to confront the fact that their child is about to be-come a sexual being."

I respectfully disagree. Peer behind the momentary di-version that an impending Bar Mitzvah supplies and what you see aren't the vagaries of sex, but the finality of death.

## East Northport: Summer 1991

There was one synagogue whose name kept cropping up like a hot new actress in the gossip columns. Kehillath Shalom, which means "community of peace," was a small congregation in Cold Spring Harbor to which many of our Jewish friends belonged. That it was a Reconstructionist congregation meant nothing to me; much more significant was the fact that it was a twenty-five-minute drive from our house, clearly too long a ride to under-take on a regular basis—for Hebrew school, in any event. Nonetheless, one June afternoon, Ben having been promoted to fourth grade, Jake still in diapers, we drove there.

"This is it?" Ben asked as we slowed down. I didn't blame him for being surprised. The building across Goose Hill Road from the library was an old white clapboard house with peeling paint and a sagging porch. We pulled into the unpaved parking lot and knocked on the door, the wooden planks beneath us creaking with our weight.

A smiling, portly man wearing Bermuda shorts, a polo shirt, aviator glasses, yarmulke, and a full beard opened the door and introduced himself as Rabbi Schwartz. He welcomed us in and took us on a tour of the building with the somewhat abstract air of someone who is called upon to wear too many hats. The sanctuary was a homely, squared-off room with cracked linoleum, unappetizing tan-green paneling, and tiny windows. Near the back wall stood a jerry-built table, in front of a homemade ark holding the Torah. "This was the house John Lindsay grew up in," Rabbi Schwartz told us, walking us toward the other end of the building, which contained two small classrooms and bathrooms. "It was donated to the congregation."

I studied notices on the bulletin boards—volunteers needed to join the AIDS walk, to come to the social action committee meeting, to collect food for the community food pantry in Huntington. On the walls hung snapshots of kids and families at Hanukkah parties and Purim festivals, pasted onto oak tag, labeled with Magic Marker—pages from a homegrown album very much in progress. Through the bay window I glimpsed a garden, once elegantly landscaped but now badly overgrown, a brick patio, and a retaining wall built into a gently sloping treed hillside.

"Come up to my study," the rabbi said, leading us up a winding staircase to the second floor. We sat at a long table, and he spoke mostly to our sons, who were full of their usual exuberant questions—"Will we really learn to speak a foreign language?" "Did you read all these books?" "Why do we have to wear these little hats on our head?"

"Do *you* have any questions?" he asked, turning to my husband and me, laying his palms up on the table, a gesture inviting honesty.

"I don't really know much about Reconstructionism," I said, trying not to sound too curious.

Rabbi Schwartz handed me a brochure. "Mordecai Kaplan's version of Judaism recognizes the weight of tradition but doesn't allow the past to veto the present. That's the nuts and bolts. For details, read the brochure. Come to an adult ed class." He paused, then added, "Don't join us if you're planning on having a big Bar Mitzvah. We have room for only about a hundred people."

"That's no problem," I assured him. I liked the synagogue as much for what it didn't have—a big, fancy building, a men's club and a sisterhood, an unctuous rabbi—as for its bare-bones, no-frills, egalitarian, activist agenda. If ever a synagogue existed that I could consider joining, this was it. Oppositionist to its very timbers, it spoke of its refusal to be like others, of its insistence on breaking new ground. Its utter unpretentiousness, its chaotic clutter and messiness verging on semidilapidation, drew me in.

"Were your parents active in a synagogue?" he asked, surprising me.

"My father was," I said, remembering, for the first time in years, that first meeting with my father's rabbi in his study and his stern admonition to make the synagogue part of our lives. How long ago was that conversation? Let's see, it must have been 1964. My father was about to turn thirty-nine. And I was . . . thirty-nine.

"Come to services," Rabbi Schwartz invited us, a prelude to good-bye. "Check us out. See what you think." He rose, placed his hands on the boys' heads to center their yarmulkes, and saw us out.

"I don't have to go to services," I said to my husband on the ride home. Driving thirty minutes to synagogue on Friday nights or Saturday mornings was not an appealing prospect. In my grandparents' time, they had simply to throw on their coats and head out the door for the five-minute walk to their shul, their "stebel," as it was called—a tiny, closet-size storefront synagogue within hollering distance of four or five others. In the old country, on the Lower East Side, the geography of worship dictated that you lived within walking distance of your house of prayer, that it formed the hub of your neighborhood; in fact, the word "parish" derives from *paroikia,* the Greek word for neighborhood. Only in twentieth-century America did we begin to define our communities by philosophical like-mindedness rather than physical proximity.

"I know all the Judaism I need to know," I continued, as if David were challenging me. I sounded angry but wasn't sure why. The synagogue itself seemed very promising, all I could ask it to be. But in my heart of hearts I think I felt defeated. I was making an admission, long in coming, that I was unable, on my own, to give my children the kind of Jewish education I had, a tactile, visceral, aromatic Judaism that seeps in through your pores as much as your ears and eyes. Sure, I could raise them to be ethical, moral people, to be generous, bighearted, and courageous. We already read Bible stories, talked about the Golden Rule, and invoked the metaphor that humankind is a bigger version of our immediate family, that we're all responsible for each other, that we make sacrifices for the larger good while at the same time being careful not to neglect ourselves.

But I wished for one moment that my sons could witness their great-grandmothers lighting Shabbos candles, waving their fingers over the flames as if defying God to burn them; I wished they could see the crowded seder tables they set, the Yiddish they spoke; witness their insistence on not driving or writing on Shabbos, on keeping meat and dairy separate in the kitchen—bacon and ham as fearful as germs; be treated to the infusion, the sensory bouquet, of Judaism that I had experienced. My parents did not observe all the holidays when I was growing up, but I knew they were there, just as I knew that certain relations whom we never saw, who lived in Philadelphia, Rio, and Johannesburg, were nonetheless in our family.

My sons would never have this education. Left to my own devices, I'd pass along a scrap of my religion to my sons, just as in *Mr. Mani,* the Israeli novelist A. B. Yehoshua relates the story of a coat that is passed down through five genera-tions—a coat that once saved a man's life, but that ends up as a frayed scrap of material, from which the man's descendants have to infer the entire garment. I could mark the holidays and light the candles, but I couldn't moan the way my grand-mothers did, couldn't perform the hand dance, couldn't even cover my eyes and momentarily retreat from the room as my mother did. A slant education in Judaism wasn't avail-able to them, as it had been to me; they'd have to go the for-mal route.

"We might as well join," I said finally, letting David in on the last sentence of a long conversation with myself. For it wasn't only Judaism that I absorbed from my grandmother, that I wanted my children to learn, but the very essence of spirituality: that there are worlds we can't touch or feel—which may in fact no longer exist—that we can nonetheless visit; people we don't know who are nonetheless with us; languages we can't speak that we nonetheless understand.

"It's totally up to you," he said.

"Then let's just do it," I said, much the way you buy a sofa that converts to a bed because you foresee in the future that you might have friends spend the night, even though at the moment everyone you know lives in town.

CHAPTER 2

# *Women/Men*

**F**riday evening, 1956. Though she hates to spend Shabbos in Queens, my grandmother is with us. She misses the Bronx; it's kosher in the same way that only certain meat is. Judgmental, seated at the kitchen table, she watches as my mother, her daughter, retrieves the glass candelabrum and places it on a silver tray on the kitchen table. I get to stick two stubby white candles into the holes. My grandmother sniffs. Something's not right, though neither my mother nor I know where we went wrong.

My grandmother lights the match dangerously, drawing it toward her, not away from her, as my parents have instructed me, the flame leaping to life just beneath her nose. She touches it to both wicks, then attempts to extinguish it by shaking it. But her hand moves slowly, and her grasp on the flaming strip of cardboard between her thumb and forefinger looks less than secure. When the match is finally extinguished, she takes a deep breath, and then her hands begin moving as if they have lives of their own, fluid and graceful, independent of her stocky trunk. She waves them like a magician or a side-show freak impervious to fire, her palms closing in on the flame, her fingertips coming together as if to form the apex of a roof, the tapered, snaky blue and yellow flame a seductive belly dance undulating just beneath her palms.

Abruptly the dance stops. She cups her palms over her eyes, sways faintly, and begins intoning the ancient prayers to herself. Hers is a sadness that doesn't admit others.

"Good Shabbos," she says finally, refusing to look anyone in the eyes, as if this were between her and God.

Friday evening, 1966. I'm in the living room, studying history for a test on Monday, waiting for my father to get home. Outside, the colorless Long Island afternoon is waning. My mother, who hasn't left the kitchen since breakfast, who just put the string beans up to boil and sectioned the grapefruit halves we'll have for starters with her curved knife, consults the Jewish calendar hanging inside the broom closet. It's time to light candles. She takes her glass candelabrum from the sideboard, places it on the dining room table, strikes the match, puts her hands over her eyes, and says the prayers half-aloud. She never sways or moans or moves her hands over the flames. Then she sighs, a deep sigh, and says, "Good Shabbos," to no one in particular. From the living room, where I am in revolt against Judaism, I watch her like a spy.

Friday evening, 1993. I'm alone in the kitchen, putting the last pot away, wrapping a plate of leftovers, placing it in the fridge. David usually cooks on Friday—Chinese food one week, seafood the next, whatever he has a hankering for—which means I wash and clean up. He's upstairs now, with our sons, each in their respective rooms, amusing themselves with television, books, magazines, phone calls. Downstairs, only one light, the one directly over the table, is still on.

In a few minutes I'll retrieve the silver candlesticks, a present from my parents, and the stocky white Sabbath candles. "Boys," I'll call upstairs, my voice tentative, rising at the end. "Come on down to light candles."

They won't respond at first. I'll have to call again, and again, before they thunder down. "Can I light the match, please, please?" Ben will beg.

Lighting candles, I tell him, is a woman's job, one of the few religious responsibilities that devolve on women. I always insist on doing it. I touch the flame to the wicks, then allow the boys to blow it out. Though I remember how my grandmother's hands danced, and how my mother covered her eyes, I do neither of these. I light the candles with no ceremony at all, as if we were in the midst of a power outage and needed them for light. But I always reach out to touch my husband and sons, if only a tip of their T-shirts. Together we sing the blessing. We're supposed to sing a blessing over the challah, the traditional braided bread, and over a cup of red wine, but I have neither. We look at each other for a moment, knowing there's more, not sure what comes next. This is it? Our candle lighting feels paltry or, rather, like a perfectly serviceable coat we've been given but nonetheless feel self-conscious about wearing because we're used to something new. Then we say, "Good Shabbos," and kiss each other. Released, the boys thunder back upstairs; my husband lingers with me for a moment, then he too heads upstairs, and again I am alone.

"I've always loved coming home on Friday nights," my father told me the day before I was married, when quite by chance we found ourselves alone for a moment at the kitchen table.

"I walk into the house, everything's neat and clean, the table's nicely set, those delicious smells, the pie all juicy . . . "

I was outraged. Was this his prenuptial advice?—a paean to housework? Did he not realize how much time my mother put in cleaning the chicken, peeling and cutting the carrots and potatoes, putting out cranberry sauce, ironing the table-cloth, running out to the bakery to stand in line for the chal-lah, all those chores upon chores, innumerable items on an endless list?

Yet she never complained the way I complain about the burden of housework. To her, Friday was a day like any other, only more so. If she felt any stirring of spirituality at all, it was probably when she thought about her pies. Though she was everywhere else the kind of woman who not only made lists but placed the most unpleasant task first, to get it out of the way, or otherwise worked in strict chronology, she allowed herself, each Friday morning, to begin her day with her great-est pleasure—dessert. Immediately after shooing my sister and me out of the house and off to school, she'd take down her tin canisters of flour and sugar, the measuring spoons and cups, the spatulas with which she'd smooth off the top of the Crisco, and her red-handled pastry blender. To her the dough was alive; some weeks it was good, some weeks not—most mysteriously, she could divine instantly, even before the last of the shortening was incorporated into the dough, what the result would be. Her mood, she believed, exerted something like a tidal influence over the disposition of the dough. When a pie is in the oven, she instructed me sternly, you can't jump or run around—it affects the crust. Baking a pie was like having a baby sister in the crib; you had to curtail your natural exuberance.

But apart from her pies, her attitude toward cooking, her family, and religion was nothing if not practical. It was as if she'd inherited a puppy she hadn't asked for yet was now charged with keeping alive. Many of the rituals were empty for her, and she couldn't defend them, yet she sought to uphold them, because they mattered to her mother, to her dead father, to many people she didn't feel like betraying. Philosophically she was a Conservative Jew. For her, the challenge was to hang on to, to conserve, those elements of Judaism that had been bequeathed to her rather than to understand them, question them, adapt them to the realities of her life.

I remembered how, on Friday nights, after I refused to accompany my father to services, he would wait until dessert, until after his first bite of my mother's apple pie, redolent of cinnamon and nutmeg, to mutter that he supposed he'd head over to shul that night. We met his announcement with such stony stares that eventually he stopped telling us in advance. He'd eat his dinner, sit in his chair with the newspaper, looking as if he had all the time in the world, and then, just a few minutes before eight, he'd sigh deeply, get up, and rummage in the hall closet for his hat and coat. "I won't be long," he'd mumble, as if he were being forced out of his warm house against his will.

But we knew that he wanted to go, though he couldn't tell us why, and we knew that he knew how abandoned we felt, that the house felt hollow and unprotected without him. Something at synagogue gave him sustenance he couldn't find at home. He chose to sit and stand with other men rather than stay home with his wife and daughters.

No wonder Friday night services never tempted me. I felt most spiritual those Friday nights when I was bound up in the pleasure of my family. It was the one night of the week when we didn't have basketball games, soccer practice, PTA meetings, reading groups. A night to stay cozily at home, to walk through the living room and kitchen, lowering shades, turning off lights and securing locks as we went, picking up whatever we'd need to get through the night—newspapers, a glass of water or a cup of tea, reading glasses—retreating upstairs with all our necessities, the downstairs becoming as remote as a foreign country with each step; a night to spend time with each boy in his room, sprawled on his bed, becoming engrossed in a board game, reading, talking, and tucking him in; to finally retire to our bedroom, the inner sanctum, for a few hours of long-deserved, long-postponed, much-anticipated end-of-the-working-week conversation, sex, and sleep.

Yet I had plucked from Judaism's intricate weave a single ritual, the lighting of Sabbath candles, and seized upon it, insisted upon it—with my own modifications. For I had no Jewish calendar listing the changing times of sunset, and even if I did, I'd have ignored it. In winter it came too early; in summer, too late. Obstinately I preferred to light the candles when every chore was done—the most peaceful few moments of the week, moments I sought to prolong by not immediately summoning my family—marking the end of work, erecting a gateway to a different kind of time. Anyway, if I lit them when the law specified, they wouldn't have lasted to comfort me, the dying light snaking up the stairwell, when, in the middle of the night, I woke to go to the bathroom and check on the boys.

Doing more—going to services, as observant Jews do, as my father insisted that we do—would have interrupted all this, would have precluded it entirely. I'd have to have prepared dinner hours earlier, roused myself from the table, changed my clothes, gotten the boys cleaned up, and shepherded everyone into the car by seven-thirty in order to arrive at services by eight. These were the time constraints within which my mother, and her mother, had worked. In fact, Fridays, the blessed Sabbath, seemed at times to be nothing more than an elaborate engine stoked by women for the express purpose of pushing men out of the house toward synagogue at the appropriate time.

My father knew that a slightly different but no less valid version of services took place each Friday night in his own home—that's what he tried to tell me on the eve of my wedding—yet he couldn't trust it. He had to leave it behind to do what the rabbis told him to do, to worship as the rabbis had decreed. Women at home, men at shul. That's how it had always been.

Though Judaism shuns asceticism and wholeheartedly celebrates connubial life and the pleasures of the flesh, its orthodox spokesmen exude an unspoken bias that things can't get serious when women are around. Girls are afterthoughts; women are forbidden to stand on the *bimah,* the raised platform at the front of the synagogue where the Torah and the Eternal Light rest, or to touch the sacred text, welcomed only in the kitchen, in the back of the synagogue, in the bedroom—and then forced to endure a second insult of having these confining rooms of exile exalted by men, as if this were compensation enough. "A woman of valor, her price beyond rubies," reads a psalm included in the Friday night service—the service women are too exhausted to attend—praising the nameless, selfless wife who toils on behalf of her husband and children, who lights the candles, prepares and cleans up after meals, keeps track of *Yahrzeit* dates. How convenient to enshrine the woman you refuse to pray with, to exempt her from obeying the 613 daily commandments men must fulfill by claiming she is innately holier, more pure, pious, and spiritual than men, requiring fewer constraints, altogether closer to God.

The desertion my mother, sister, and I experienced when my father trundled off all those Friday nights to his house of worship, spurning the sacredness of home, was only partly due to his physical absence. Each in our way, we lamented his reluctance——or was it his inability?——to see past the ruse, behind the rationalization, to notice the ways in which we were left out and left behind.

"Hello, Roberta. This is Eve Lodge. I'm calling from Kehillath Shalom. Do you have a moment?"

Within a few months of joining the synagogue, I'd learned to recognize Eve's voice over the phone. In fact, she'd come to embody the synagogue; when I thought of it, I heard her. We'd never met, though she acted as if our paths had somewhere crossed. And the purpose of her calls, always placed at considerate times, just after dinner while my sons were busy with homework or reading, was to inform me, in her crisp, no-nonsense way, that a congregational meeting at which the budget would be voted upon was scheduled to take place next week. Or that the mother of one of the founding members had just died; the funeral would be on Wednesday at ten, burial at Mt. Zion Cemetery, and the family would be sitting shiva at home until Tuesday.

Her unassailable confidence that I'd be interested in and grateful for this information always made me smile. Never once did I call to her attention how preposterous it was that I needed to know about the funeral of a woman with whom I had shared no earthly connection. Perhaps Eve's earnestness deterred me. Maybe I inferred from her just-the-facts-ma'am tone that she didn't know the deceased, either, but that didn't preclude her from shouldering her congregational responsibilities. More likely I remembered the period of mourning following my father's death, when the question of who came through the open door to offer condolences—their relation to my father, the length of their relationship—didn't matter nearly as much as the fact that they had shown up. I welcomed everyone and drew comfort from them, accepted them as people who were paying tribute to my father no matter how tangentially they had known each other. When it comes to condolences, I realized during those somber eight days, volume, the sheer number of bodies, counts. Very few people can muster any words of comfort at all; in fact, often those closest to the deceased are the most tongue-tied and look to you, the mourner, to help them out. After one or two of these intense, fraught encounters with stammering, teary friends, I was ready to throw open the doors, to welcome anyone who had ever said a word to my father, or watched him mow the lawn, or sat in a room with him, or belonged, however tenuously, to an organization to which he also belonged.

For whatever odd combination of reasons, I dutifully reached for a pen and paper, took down all the facts Eve relayed in quick succession—clearly she was the kind of woman who couldn't imagine a household in which a pen and scratch pad weren't positioned near the phone—and thanked her for calling. Sometimes I told her that I'd do everything I could to try to come; sometimes I explained that because I had young children at home who needed ferrying to activities and nearly constant supervision, a husband who worked several evenings a week, my own job and various domestic responsibilities, it was often difficult for me to get out of the house on Friday night or early Sunday morning. No time was the right time; between work, family, friends, and the few minutes of leisure I could scrape together, my dance card was full. Honestly, I couldn't imagine any of my friends, or any woman I knew, being available for even one of these activities.

"Yes, dear, I understand," said Eve Lodge with earnest sincerity, sounding as though she knew that in my heart of hearts I wanted to say yes, just once, if only to repay her for her indefatigable kindness even in the face of my constant rejection, even though by now she must have surmised that I'd never attend anything. And sure enough, a week or two later, Eve would call again, with more news. She wasn't angry or resentful. In fact, she sounded hopeful each time, as if maybe this would prove the charm. "Here's an event designed just for people in your situation," she began. "It's our monthly 'Sunday the Rabbi Eats Early'—a potluck supper at the synagogue with the rabbi, a family event. Just bring a dish and come prepared to talk."

"You're a one-woman sisterhood," I said to her, as I dutifully wrote down the time and date and then balled up the piece of paper—as if I'd ever give up my Sunday afternoon date with my crossword puzzle and our Sunday night family pizza dinner to drive to the synagogue and talk about theological issues over someone else's warmed-over casserole with a group of total strangers.

"Oh, we don't have a sisterhood. That was something this congregation decided at the outset. No sisterhood, no men's club. We'd all work together. Our committee is called the Caring Community."

"Are there men on your committee?" I asked.

"Why, no, not at the moment."

Not ever, I thought to myself. Maybe Kehillath Shalom wasn't as different from my father's suburban Jewish center as I wanted to believe.

"But why do I have to go to Hebrew school?" Ben whined from the backseat. I glanced at the car clock—three forty-five. Just one hour ago he'd returned home from school, had a hasty snack, finished his math handout, found his Hebrew books (one in his closet, one in his brother's room), completed his Hebrew homework, and climbed reluctantly into the car.

We were on the short stretch our family had dubbed Roller Coaster Road, thanks to two stomach-lurching crests followed by sharp turns. I always drove faster than the speed limit in the hope that some of the thrill of getting to Hebrew school would linger once Ben was in the classroom.

"You have to go," I began, trying to guess how many times we'd had this conversation, as we turned onto the street that would take us past two other synagogues into historic Huntington, "because Daddy and I want you to learn about your heritage."

"Did you go to Hebrew school?" Jake, age three, piped up from the backseat.

"No, I didn't, but Daddy did. And he had a Bar Mitzvah, and we want you to have one, too."

"Why didn't you have a Bar Mitzvah?" Ben asked.

The more problematic a discussion, the more likely my family is to conduct it in the car. Maybe being released from having to make eye contact helps; I'm not sure. But having been called on to explain how the baby gets inside in the first place while waiting on line in the supermarket, and to answer whether or not I ever tried any illegal drugs while helping Ben try on bathing suits in a crowded fitting room, I found this question less threatening, if a bit more theoretical.

"Many girls didn't have Bat Mitzvahs in those days," I explained, feeling as if I were relating events dating from the Pleistocene era. In fact, the first Bat Mitzvah wasn't celebrated until 1922, when Mordecai Kaplan, Reconstructionism's founder, celebrated his own daughter's. "Anyway," I added, "Grandma didn't like the synagogue in our neighborhood."

"What was wrong with it?" Jake piped up.

Suddenly I wished I had a movie of my life, so he could see the images that rose to my mind. It's Yom Kippur, the Day of Atonement, and my mother always wakes up in a grim mood. She puts on her gray suit, the one she bought on Division Street, and a subdued floral blouse. We walk with her across the park I can see from my bedroom window, as if we are going to the supermarket. Around the corner from the kosher deli, on a shady, narrow side street, in a little, two-story house, is the shul you have to know about—there's no sign labeling it as such. People mill about outside, mostly women in fancy hats and children in crisp, starched outfits, and a few wrinkled men looking as if they slept in their clothes. My sister and I are also dressed up; for the High Holy Days we get new suits, dresses, coats, shoes, even gloves and pocketbooks. My father looks as if we are going to a restaurant, wearing a suit and tie and overcoat.

My mother adjusts the veil of her hat and tells my father she won't be long. I want to go inside, too. Reluctantly she agrees. We walk into a tiny, dark foyer and then into a big room. Rows and rows of women, their heads covered, sit together, the rows too cramped to cross your legs. In front of us, a few rows ahead, hangs a dingy white curtain, like those in the fitting rooms of department stores, which blocks our sight. But I hear the sound of men milling about, the undercurrent of their voices. There's singing, too, coming from their part of the room. "I want to go on the other side of the curtain," I tell my mother.

"You can't," she says. "We have to stay here."

I pick up a book; it's entirely in Hebrew. The women sing the way my grandmother does, without words. We stand up and sit down. I drop the book on the floor. "Go outside to your father," my mother tells me. "I'll be out soon."

My sister is climbing up and down the steps leading to the building, her gloves dirty, her shoes scuffed, and I join her. My father leans against a straggly tree in brilliant sunshine and consults his watch every few minutes until my mother emerges. I can tell from the way she shades her eyes with her gloved hand that she has a headache, and she'll claim that it's from not eating, from standing in that smelly room, from sitting down and standing up, from the incessant muttering and moaning. But I think she feels ill because she has spent too much time in a place where she isn't wanted, has been made to feel like a gate crasher in her own religion. I never want to go back, never—not until they let me see what's on the other side of the curtain.

In the Conservative synagogue my parents joined on Long Island no curtain separated the men's from the women's section, but the extent to which women were excluded from Judaism's sacred places was reinforced countless ways, year after year. Each spring, at Passover, we gathered around the seder table and read from the Haggadah, the book that tells of the Exodus from Egypt. Even as a child I objected to the parable of the four sons. " 'Son' stands for 'child,' " my father told me, an explanation I pretended to accept. Likewise, when we prayed, "God of our fathers," we were supposedly implicitly referring to our mothers as well. Only gradually had I realized that these texts implied no such generalization, that they were horrifyingly literal: no girls were mentioned during the Passover story, or in the daily or Sabbath prayer books, because none of the rabbis had bothered to notice them.

In her book *Standing Again at Sinai: Judaism from a Feminist Perspective,* Judith Plaskow explores "the questions" that "emerge out of a contradiction between the holes in the text and the felt experience of many Jewish women." The text she refers to is Exodus 19:15, in which Moses is told, "Be ready for the third day; do not go near a woman"—leading scholars to infer that when the Jewish people gathered at Sinai to receive the law, only men were present. "For if Moses' words come as a shock and an affront," Plaskow continues, "it is because women have always known or assumed our presence at Sinai; the passage is painful because it seems to deny what we have always taken for granted. Of course we were at Sinai; how is it then that the text could imply we were not there?"

It's entirely to my mother's credit, I thought, halfway to Huntington, that she didn't send me to Hebrew school at the Orthodox shul, where questions like these had no answers, were generations away from being posed.

But what would she have done if I had been a boy? Incredible, that this question had never occurred to me before. Surely she would have felt obliged to launch me on a course of study leading to my Bar Mitzvah; not to do so would have been unthinkable. Of course, had I been a boy, I'd have been sitting in front of the curtain. Would I have thought about the girls behind me, in the smaller classroom, who learned Hebrew letters and the basic prayers but never went near the Torah?

"Well, I hate coming," Ben said, his voice becoming more emphatic as we neared our destination. What I couldn't tell him was that I hated the trip as well. I hated walking into the crowded lobby, seeing all the signs for AIDS walks and Succoth dinners and Sunday morning book groups; I hated being called by class mothers, so much more demanding than Eve Lodge, who asked if I would bake cakes for Saturday morning services, help decorate the *sukkah,* plan the Hanukkah party. Was there no end to their requests? I felt as if I were being assaulted, as if our family were being asked to give up our private time in the name of Judaism.

"I'm sorry, I can't," I had said over and over again, wishing I could hang up on them or cry, "Leave me alone!" What was wrong with all these people—didn't they have a life? All I wanted, as far as Judaism was concerned, was for my son to learn about his history, his heritage, to know who he was and the stock he came from. I wanted him to have an opportunity to meet other Jewish kids. To learn how to get through a service. To learn what he needed so he could celebrate his Bar Mitzvah. So we could discharge our obligation to our family.

And I wanted to be left out of it.

Yet no sooner did we pull into the synagogue parking lot than Ben's resistance—and mine—seemed to melt away. Afraid that he was late, he popped out of the car, waited impatiently while I extricated Jacob from his car seat, and waved to kids as we walked across the street, up the crumbling path and sagging steps to where Rabbi Schwartz stood in the doorway, greeting everyone.

I too felt calmer now that we were here. Walking Ben to his classroom, makeshift as it was, meeting in the sanctuary for lack of space, I smiled at those moms I recognized, wondering which one had called the other night to recruit me for a task. They had every right to ask. They weren't faceless telemarketers calling during dinner—they were members of

a group I had willingly joined. They were asking me to contribute more than lip service to my son's religious education,
to follow through on the commitment I'd made when I
joined the synagogue. Maybe they knew something I didn't.
Maybe they'd found a way to integrate their home and synagogue life in a way I couldn't yet imagine. They seemed to
have time for everything; to feel, within this hive of activity,
very much at ease and in charge, at home. Perhaps, I re-
flected, their concept of family wasn't as narrow as mine.

"Your father's *Yahrzeit* will be commemorated on June 10,
corresponding to Sivan 28. Light the candle on the evening
before. You may wish to make a contribution to the synagogue in his memory." The postcard was signed by the Caring Community.

I was taken aback by it, almost affronted by this blatant
presumption of intimacy. How did they know this?

My husband reminded me that upon joining the synagogue, we had been asked to fill out a lengthy questionnaire
on which we listed our Hebrew names and the dates family
members had died. Imagine, strangers keeping track of this
bank of personal information. Perhaps Eve had sent the
card; she, I recalled, was a member of the Caring Commu-

nity. Maybe this intrusion was in fact as benign as one of her calls, a gentle way of letting me know that as prodigal as I might be, as petulant and noncommittal, someone was still watching over me, keeping track of my obligations even if I wasn't.

It had been five years since my father had died, at home, in his bedroom, in the house he'd loved, tended, and improved for almost a quarter century. Once he'd spent a weekend on his knees, laying flagstone tiles in the foyer and hallway; a week before his death, he could barely walk, even with a walker, the few feet from bedroom to kitchen. "I never realized how long it was," he told me, collapsing into a kitchen chair.

Friends who had sustained their own losses assured me that after a while the images of his illness would recede and that I'd remember him as he'd been for most of his life— hale, tall, strong. This turned out to be only partly true. I had a clear picture of him standing on the front steps of the house as my husband, son, and I swung our car into the driveway for a visit, and how he would stand there again to prolong saying good-bye; most often he had his arm around my mother, and they were both waving.

But another image persisted. I saw him, at the end of what proved to me a long remission, stumbling into the dining room—we thought he was suffering from simple back pain, but in reality he had a spinal tumor—to light a *Yahrzeit* candle for his father, who had died nine years earlier. My grandfather Murray had had no use for Judaism or any religion. He said heretical things at every opportunity and tweaked my grandmother for her piety. He never said a Yiddish word, never went to synagogue except under duress, wore a yarmulke grudgingly at other people's sons' Bar Mitzvahs. Yet here was his son dutifully lighting a candle, just as nine years ago he had dutifully recited Kaddish at the synagogue every night for eleven months. I watched him strike the match, touch the flame to the wick, thinking how strange it was that my pious father intoning prayers for his godless father would not, in death, be repaid in kind.

This candle lighting—and fainting at the kitchen table when I was eight years old, and having to be helped to bed by my mother—were the only womanly things I'd ever witnessed my father do. Maybe that's why both stuck in my mind so stubbornly.

I'd always imagined that he'd gone about learning about his religion, when he turned forty, with the same purpose, devotion to rationality, and single-minded vigor he brought to this job. Each stride he took into the life of his suburban synagogue took him further away from the messy mumbojumbo of his mother's religion, a swirling miasma of oldworld superstition, fears, *bobe mayses,* or grandmother's stories. Enough patchwork Judaism, he'd decided; enough meandering seders at my grandmother's house, during which we read the story of the Exodus from Egypt in fits and starts, everyone on a different page, the children clamoring for food, my grandfather refusing to read another word until he had his soup—enough!

If you want to be religious, then you go to shul; if you want to have an impact, you don't join committees like Eve's and work behind the scenes, you head, like a heat-seeking arrow, for the beating heart of the enterprise—you go to services, you sit in the sanctuary reading the prayer book, you look at the ark containing the Torah beneath the Eternal Light. My father made himself understand it all, from the outside in. One Passover he staged a coup, moving the seder from my grandmother's house to ours, where he installed himself at the head of our table, put on a yarmulke, and told us all to get to work. He didn't know the prayers or any of the music; he couldn't sing; he had no sense of the recursiveness of the mealtime service, that you could repeat everything, a prayer or song, that each person could read a section and ask questions. To him, the Haggadah was simply a book, and when you read a book you started at the beginning and went until the end. This meal, I realized, was a turning point in the religious history of our family. We were in the process of recapitulating the development of religion in our culture, having moved, in the space of a generation, from a primitive, mystical matriarchy to an enlightened logical patriarchy.

Yet at the end of his life, when he hadn't the strength to lift the prayer book, much less go to services, he prayed at home. And on one of my last visits, when I walked into his bedroom on a Saturday morning to find the prayer book splayed open on his chest and asked if he wanted me to read from it or if I should just hold it for him, he shook his head no and made a face, as if to say, That old thing. Just put it off to the side. I don't need it anymore.

At first I took this to mean he'd renounced it all—that the glaring incandescence of mortality burned away all the accoutrements of faith. But later I realized that he'd simply reverted to the brand of religion he'd known as a child, his mother's sense of religion, in which mystery and faith existed all around him, one for which he was no longer the driving force, but simply a beneficiary—a religion in which his mother, wife, and daughters were as welcomed as his rabbi and cantor, equally important, equally necessary.

"The Social Action Committee will meet on Tuesday evening, at 7:30 P.M. at the synagogue, to discuss our affiliating with Habitat for Humanity. For more information, call Vicki Lens."

This item in the synagogue newsletter caught my eye. A few typewritten pages that arrived every month, filled with words from the president, the rabbi, Jewish news from around the world, and lists and lists of future activities—book groups, canoe trips, breakfasts, hiking expeditions, communal dinners—it was the written equivalent of Eve's calls. I usually kept it around for a few days so I could glance at it when I had a minute and nothing else at hand to read—while waiting for the spaghetti water to boil, for example.

The Social Action Committee. What an optimistic name. The last time I'd become involved in any substantive social action was in 1968, during my junior year of high school, when my friends and I canvassed for Eugene McCarthy. We'd meet and hang out together at his campaign headquarters, a storefront squeezed between a drugstore and supermarket in a shopping center backing on the train station. It was the year that Robert Kennedy and Martin Luther King Jr. had been shot.

The evening of King's assassination I'd been sitting in a class at the synagogue, the only religious class I ever took, taught by an Orthodox rabbi from Queens who schlepped out to Long Island on Thursday nights one spring to teach suburban Jewish girls about Jewish family life.

We'd abandoned the curriculum that night—the laws governing sexual intercourse seemed beside the point as news of riots and fires in Detroit and Washington came over the little radio he had propped up on his desk. Rabbi Witty, a heavyset man I liked despite myself, seemed more concerned with the looting than with the fact that a great leader had been gunned down. My friends and I grew disgusted with his narrow perspective and couldn't wait to leave, couldn't wait for school the next day so we could meet with our like-minded teachers and friends.

By coincidence, a theater group had been scheduled to appear at school the next day, and the play they put on was about race relations in America. "Oh freedom," the largely black cast sang at the end of the play, to a sea of white faces, all of us in tears. "Oh freedom, oh freedom over me. And before I'll be a slave I'll be buried in my grave, and go home to my Lord, and be free."

Since then I'd attended anti–Vietnam War marches in Washington, circulated petitions, supported causes—but never with the same intensity. The personal overtook the political. In some deep part of myself I knew that I needed to get my own house in order—to create a family, find work, create a network of friends. And even after I'd done that I hesitated. Sure, I'd send money to environmental organizations, join the writers' union, dash off letters to congressional leaders. But when asked to donate my time I answered the same way I had Eve Lodge: Sorry, none available. I disliked committee meetings. Nothing ever got done, and you were held captive to people with massive ego problems. I didn't know the lingo, couldn't muster the patience.

Still . . . social action. I cut out the box with the pertinent facts and affixed it to the fridge. I'd think about it.

"Oh, hi," Vicki Lens said after I identified myself as a new member of the congregation interested in joining her committee. She sounded as if my call had made her day. "We meet just before the board meeting, so you can stay for that, too, if you like." We determined that we lived just a few minutes away from each other; she offered to pick me up and drive me to the meeting. I thanked her but said I'd drive myself. Staying for a board meeting wasn't something I was ready to sign on for.

I was unexpectedly nervous driving down Roller Coaster Road the night of the meeting, unused to being alone and to negotiating the twists and turns without the benefit of daylight. My kids hadn't been happy to see me go; my husband said, "Good luck," when I said good-bye, as if I were embarking on an adventure. If he harbored any skepticism, he kept it to himself. What would my father say if he could see me?

I parked the car and crossed Goose Hill Road to the synagogue. It seemed deserted. The voices and tumult of children who had recently filled the yard, entering and leaving Hebrew school, lingered in the shadows. I felt as if I were showing up for a party that had already ended.

Four people—two men, two women—sat around a long table in the synagogue sanctuary when I opened the door. Vicki Lens, a pretty, dark-haired woman about my age, rose to introduce herself and shake my hand. "Welcome to the Social Action Committee," she said, indicating the others. She and I were the youngest members by many years.

Vicki explained, for my benefit, that the committee's primary responsibility was to decide among which worthy causes to disperse the funds in its budget, but that tonight's meeting was special: a representative from Habitat for Humanity had been invited to describe his organization and ask us if we were interested in affiliating. Ours was the first Long Island synagogue Habitat had approached.

Committee members thanked our guest, raised questions, debated fine points—everyone, it seemed, had something to say except for me. Against the backdrop of these deliberations, other people began filing into the sanctuary and took seats around the rectangular tables clumped together in the center of the room. They looked weary, after a day of work, but comfortable, in their element. One man in particular reminded me of my father, who used to collect his papers and slip into his jacket on his way out to a meeting at the synagogue with a resigned, "Someone's got to do it, and it might as well be me" look.

As they took their seats, the Social Action Committee finished its deliberations, voting unanimously to recommend to the board that we affiliate with Habitat.

With that, the members of the Social Action Committee rose, pushed their table over to the cluster of tables in the center of the sanctuary, and took seats for the board meeting. I was asked—very politely—to take a seat off to the side, where I was welcome to watch the board's proceedings. Mostly I watched the president, a tall and regal, well-dressed woman with stylishly coiffed gray hair who presided over the meeting with a deftness that bespoke deep-seated confidence, as if she'd chaired many meetings in the past. Yet she spoke from the heart, without a hint of bureaucratese, as if she were entertaining a few close friends in her living room.

If I closed my eyes, I could imagine us around a seder table. In fact, the meeting reminded me of a seder I'd once attended with the Orthodox family of my college boyfriend. His aunt lived in a small Manhattan apartment into which nearly thirty people gathered and found a sliver of a place at a table that stretched from one end of the living room to the other. It was a raucous group, noisy and opinionated; at times it sounded as if five seders were taking place simultaneously, everyone talking, expounding, singing, praying, noshing, drinking, arguing. I'd never before encountered such a spunky, feisty, exuberant version of Judaism.

The board meeting, too, was lively and cacophonous. I relished the presence of women—not just taking notes and serving coffee, but presiding, heading committees, disputing arguments, lobbying for a motion, the way Vicki did when she recommended that we join with Habitat for Humanity. Sparks flew. "This is a Christian ministry," one board member exclaimed, outraged. "Read their mission statement."

"They build their houses on Saturday," said another. "We can't work on Saturday." The discussion verged on chaos, yet the president let everyone speak, allowing opposing opinion to emerge without quashing anyone, as if she were a surfer and knew how to ride the wave.

Finally, although she looked as if she had plenty to say herself, she recognized the rabbi. "Look, folks," he began, turning sideways in his chair, his upturned palms like trays on a scale on which he was weighing options. "There's no reason for them not to use Christian language; until now it's been a Christian group, churches only. But we all agree on the cause, and on the integrity this organization has shown, and on their ability to accomplish its task. So why don't we ask them if they'd change the language for us? If they'd take 'Christ' out of their statement. If they'd sponsor a work crew on Sunday, when we could work. We could ask. What have we got to lose?"

Relative silence. No loud objections, no angry voices. Vicki Lens said that she would personally contact the director of Habitat and see if we could hammer out a compromise. The president called for a vote, though she already knew the outcome. Sure enough, the board endorsed a tentative affiliation with Habitat pending the changes the rabbi had suggested. "And we're adjourned," the president said.

It was nearly eleven o'clock. Some people left the room immediately, but many more lingered, standing around in groups in the sanctuary, in the vestibule, on the porch, the steps, as if they couldn't bring themselves to leave. They talked and talked, their voices rising and falling as the minutes ticked by. I lingered, too, moving from group to group, trying to find a way into a conversation. I wanted to say good-bye to Vicki Lens, to ask if Eve Lodge was here.

Mostly I wanted to introduce myself to the president of the board and tell her that I never saw anyone so confidently chair a meeting or withstand such a threatening level of chaos with such equanimity. Calmly in command, she seemed to combine the best traits of my mother and father into one resolute presence. I was in awe of her.

I also wanted to approach the rabbi, though he probably didn't remember me, and tell him how much I admired him. How remarkable I found it that he hadn't issued a call to circle the wagons, to draw his religion around him as a barrier, to ward off the rest of the world. Yet neither had he agreed to assimilation. We'd love to join with Habitat, he'd said, but under certain conditions. Instead of backing away entirely, he endorsed it, while voicing his qualifications. I'd never seen a rabbi react with such clearheaded ecumenism.

Waiting for Vicki to finish her conversation, to have a word with her before we drove home, I picked up a copy of a prayer book stacked in piles on a table near the sanctuary and began, in a desultory way, to flip through the pages, stopping when I came to the *Amidah,* the prayer of silent devotion. A two-part list in the middle of the page caught my eye: on the left appeared the names of the patriarchs, Abraham, Isaac, and Jacob, and opposite them, sharing the genealogical stage, given a prominence I'd never before witnessed, their wives— Sarah, Rebekah, Rachel, and Leah.

Reading these few syllables of women's names, this short list, this meager roll call, spawned a catenation of maternal images and sensations—the feel of my grandmother's roughened palm caressing my cheeks; the sight of her hunched over the wooden board on which she rolled out dough; the sound of her wordless melodies—that in turn whisked me back through time, to my earliest mothers, Sarah in the tent, Rachel at the well, going about the business of everyday life.

Sure, I knew there were women in the Bible—Queen Esther, the wife of Jael, Bathsheba, Jezebel, Deborah—but these women were held up for their wisdom or beauty, their cleverness and ferocity, their ingenuity and courage. In fact, the only reason I knew their names was precisely because of how they stood out. They were the tokens, much the same way choral directors of every chorus in which I've ever sung felt compelled to leaven a Christmas program with one or two Hanukkah songs.

To see matriarch yoked to patriarch was like finding the one small task you had to accomplish—smoothing out a bedspread, placing your special morning coffee mug in the china closet, memorizing your phone number—that made your new house feel less like a shelter and more like home. Sarah, Rebekah, Rachel, Leah—nowhere in the Bible do they speak for themselves, but in this prayer book they arose from dusty oblivion to take their rightful places alongside their spouses.

"Where are you?" God asks Abraham in Genesis, and

Abraham replies, famously, *"Hineni"*—"I am here." For the first time in my life I heard a woman's voice supply the answer: the voices of my maternal predecessors—Amelia and Matla; Rose and Sarah, my great-grandmothers; Ella and Fannie, my grandmothers; Rae, my mother. Their innumerable, whispered conversations filled my ears.

The prayer book I held in my hand, which without fanfare paired husband and wife, exposed the reality: we have always been here, shoulder to shoulder with our male partners, but we never stood together in the same room with equal comfort, with a shared sense of belonging. No wonder the Social Action Committee was the bait that had lured me out of the sanctuary of my home. Yes, I could observe the Sabbath at home as well as in shul, but sometimes we need to emerge from our houses, to come together, as men and women, to worship, to publicly affirm our affiliation and like-mindedness, and to effect political, social, and economic change. The effort required a commitment to succor and justice and equal helpings of empathy and a determination to make things happen—a perfect blend of male and female energies as we've been socialized to define them. Here, at Kehillath Shalom, a tiny congregation espousing a nascent version of Judaism struggling to be heard, I found not merely a welcome, but recognition in the deepest, most heartfelt sense.

I closed the book, replaced it on the pile, and started down the steps and across the dark path leading to the road. "Well, what did you think?" Vicki Lens asked, coming up behind me. "Did you enjoy the meeting?"

I told her that I did. And I asked her about the congregation—how it got started. "I don't know too much," she explained, only that it had split off from a larger, Conservative synagogue in Huntington over a dispute involving whether or not an antiwar speaker should be allowed to address the congregation. This was in 1968. A small cadre of families followed the rabbi, whose belief that a social and political agenda belonged squarely on the *bimah* had cost him his contract, to found their own synagogue, their own Community of Peace. An heiress had donated this building. And here we stood. "I wish I knew more," she said, "but we're new members."

"We are, too," I said. "When did you join?"

"Just six months ago," she said, opening her car door. We had parked next to each other. I'd been a member far longer than that. How had she become so involved? Her day didn't have more hours in it than mine did—she had a daughter and a full-time job as an attorney. Where did she find the time? What motivated her?

"You know everyone," I said, getting into my car.

"You will, too," she said. "Look at this, we could have driven here together after all."

"Next time," I said without thinking.

"Fine," Vicki replied through her car window. "I'll call you."

I started the engine and followed her toward Roller Coaster Road.

# CHAPTER 3

# Certainty/
# Uncertainty

 have no idea what time it is—my bedroom has no clock, and my wristwatch, tucked inside my top dresser drawer, does not light up at night—but I know it's very late. My sister, a few feet away from me, in her twin bed, is fast asleep. My parents are in bed, too, their door shut. My mind is like a car that's idling too high; I can't turn it off. Fear keeps me awake, makes me restless under the covers, turns my body hot and cold, both at the same time, makes me breathe in and out quickly, like a dog. I think about blackness, the blackness I imagine you see after you're dead. No one has ever talked to me about death. The only person I knew who has died is my grandfather, my mother's father, Raphael Engelberg, for whom I am named. He died before I

was born, before my parents were married. His oil portrait hangs in my grandmother's apartment. He's wearing a blue suit and red tie; his dark hair is tinged with gray around his ears, and he looks stern. I wish I knew more about him, but each time I ask my mother or grandmother their faces tighten as if I am hurting them. They never talk about him, but I know when they think about him—when they light candles, or dress to go to synagogue.

These nights when I can't sleep, I see myself on a gigantic Ferris wheel at Kiddie City, my favorite local amusement park, which never stops to let on new riders. It's night; the sky is dark, and the lights in the park don't reach as high as the Ferris wheel at the apogee of its turn. The spinning ride reminds me of the planets in their orbit around the sun and of the gears in a watch, all different sizes, which turn at different rates, some fast, some slow, like those on the charm of my favorite bracelet. As we spin around without stopping I try to shout to the people I can see scurrying around on the ground. They are a horde of my descendants—not my children, but my great-grandchildren and great-great-grandchildren. I shout until I'm hoarse; I want them to look up and see me, I want simply to see their faces, I want them to hear me.

"Hear, O Israel, the Lord our God, the Lord is One." This prayer, the Shema, is the holiest of all, the one repeated in every service, the prayer that is on the lips of Jewish martyrs when they die. "Hear, O Israel"—not see, for sound is more inescapable than vision, speech a form of disembodied touch, a primal connection.

But I know, as a child, shanghaied by waking nightmares in my own bed, bathed in sweat, even as my fear becomes so unbearable that I have to rouse myself, knock on the closed door of my parents' bedroom and pretend I am thirsty, even as I sip the cup of water my father brings to my bedside, that no matter how loudly I scream no one will hear, that in death you lose your voice.

My most fervent childhood prayer is for God to prevent death—my sister's, my parents'. Each night I check my sister while she sleeps by putting my hand under her nose to feel her breath. Those few nights when my parents go out, shopping or to a movie, I stand waiting at their bedroom window, which overlooks the driveway to the underground garage, straining for the first glimpse of their headlights. My grandmother pleads with me to go back to bed. "What can happen to them?" she asks, wringing her hands. Her question stymies me. She, better than anyone, should know about unseen dangers. So I stand there, at the window, shivering with fear, imagining them dead on the road, and I pray to God to return them to me and I'd be good, I wouldn't fight with my sister anymore, I'd listen to them.

God looks like the picture of Moses, with his white beard, clutching the Ten Commandments in his left hand, sitting on a throne of clouds, that adorns the cover of the book of Bible stories my grandmother reads to me, a cross between Zeus and the Pharaohs. I know He doesn't really dwell in the sky; I know He doesn't really hear me. He doesn't even blink when I pour out my heart to Him.

Finally, after what feels like hours, I see the first hint of headlights and then the familiar Chevrolet hove into view. Yet as I dive back into bed, faking sleep, praying that my grandmother won't tell on me as she always does, I know it isn't God who returned them to me but my father, an excellent driver.

They never talk about God. In our family, God's presence was one in a long list of subjects implied but never explicated. In a funny way, God's existence was a kind of absence, which matched my idea of religion—the only certainty in negation: the foods you couldn't eat, the things you couldn't do on holidays or Shabbos.

We did devote a lot of time to discussing character, doing the right thing, adhering to the Golden Rule, being honest, ethical, and moral. These were expected, at all times. Someone was looking over your shoulder even when you thought you were alone. I never felt alone. I felt as if someone were watching me; in fact—and this is a secret I didn't tell anyone, for I was afraid I'd be laughed at—I felt as if someone were filming me at all times. When I was with other people, at school or with friends, I forgot about it. But when I was alone, writing at my desk, riding my bike, sitting and looking out the window, I imagined a camera was trained on me, as if everything I did were being evaluated for rectitude and grace. And I found myself wondering, forty years later, whether this wasn't my first homespun understanding of God.

In the middle of May 1993, I phoned the rabbi of our synagogue. "My son Ben turns thirteen in January 1995," I began tentatively, queasily. Talking about dates so far in the future brought on the same touch of nausea that I experienced in my local food warehouse contemplating industrial-size containers of mayonnaise, ketchup, and Italian salad dressing. "But we were wondering if we could schedule his Bar Mitzvah for sometime in the spring so we can have an outdoor party, if that's okay. I mean, I'm not sure if it's possible to—"

*"Mazel tov!"* he bellowed, cutting me off before I could explain any further.

I was taken aback. This was a call I'd delayed placing for months. That Ben would have a Bar Mitzvah seemed a certainty—I felt an obligation to my family, to the notion of heritage. Yet if pressed to explain why he needed to undergo this ritual, or what my own need was, I wouldn't have known where to begin. On top of these purely religious concerns, planning parties was an area in which I had no expertise, and having to cut my teeth on a Bar Mitzvah seemed impossibly daunting.

But the rabbi's hearty *"Mazel tov"* halted my litany of questions and insecurities and focused me on the heart of the matter: my firstborn child, my beautiful son Benjamin, was about to come of age in the Jewish religion, to be called to the Torah and take his place with his forebears.

"Now, let's find a date," the rabbi continued. I could hear him thumbing through his appointment book. I asked for a Saturday in April, but every date was already claimed. He rifled through page after page, muttering to himself about Torah portions and Passover. "How's June third?" he finally offered.

"I'll take it," I said, feeling as if it were the last pie on the bakery shelf.

"Good," he said, and if I hadn't interrupted him, he would have hung up within a second.

"That's it?" I felt panic-stricken. Didn't I have to sign something? "What do I do now?"

"Save your money." He laughed. "Keep sending your boy to Hebrew school. Make up a guest list. What else should there be to do? You'll survive. Everyone does."

"I don't know," I said. Hanging up the phone, I felt as if I'd just begun the proverbial thousand-step journey, only for some inexplicable reason I'd forgotten how to walk.

Conversations with other rabbis had always been airless; each word they uttered, I felt, drained oxygen from the air. Talking to Rabbi Schwartz was like being in a room with a view. He'd never ask an embarrassing question, nor would he rivet you with an icy stare designed to penetrate to the depths of your being, to take your spiritual temperature—that, he indicated, was very much your business, not his. He was, in his general demeanor, a much more "I'm here if you need me" kind of fellow.

He reminded me, curiously, of Ben's first pediatrician. Though David and I had interviewed a number of doctors well in advance of my delivery date, many of whom were touchingly avuncular and heavily credentialed, we decided upon Max, who was roughly a contemporary, had young children of his own, and couldn't afford to patronize us. We could easily imagine that in the dead of night, pacing the house with his own scrawny, screaming baby in his arms, Max would be just as scared, if not quite as clueless, as we were.

As it turned out, this doctor saw us through our first medical crisis as parents. When Ben was only four days old, his bilirubin began rising precipitously. We rushed him to the hospital for some definitive tests. Sitting in a rocking chair, trying to nurse an infant who seemed to be turning more yellow with each passing moment, I said to Max, "Is he going to die?"

"I don't think so," he said, looking me right in the eye. It wasn't only his unflinching honesty that struck me to the core, but his willingness to take my concern seriously, to not dismiss it with an equivocating, "What are you talking about? Of course he'll be fine. Don't get histrionic on me."

Max's blunt honesty would have discomfited my parents as much as it comforted me. When it came to the "evil eye," my parents were as European as their great-grandparents— what you don't say aloud doesn't exist. Feeling much more modern, I'd sought out a modern doctor, and a modern rabbi, just as my parents, and theirs before them, had sought out healers of the body and mind who were their age. Until now, however, I hadn't realized that my father chose a rabbi who was his contemporary—probably because the rabbi had worked so hard to assume the mien of an older, wiser man, one to whom others deferred, the very deferral adding years to his bearing. Rabbi Schwartz didn't want to seem older than his age, thank you very much. He had a daughter only a year younger than Ben.

"June third, nineteen ninety-five," I told my mother, in-laws, sister, closest friends. "Save the date." It sounded as preposterously futuristic as the year 2000.

"My God, Ben's Bar Mitzvah? *Already?*" they asked, writing down the date in their long-range calendars. Ben was the oldest grandchild, the oldest child in our circle of friends. The fact of his imminent ascension to adolescence caught us all short. In my family's astonishment I detected a wistful note, but my friends sounded panicked. My phone call was an alarm, a wake-up call piercing a long sleep: if Ben was approaching thirteen, then their children weren't far behind. And that meant that certain long-standing, open-ended questions—whether or not to join a church or synagogue, and if so, which one, and when—needed concrete answers. Suddenly we were all thrust into a version of "The Ant and the Grasshopper," trying to prepare for a future that, though too far off to see, was nevertheless barreling our way.

"I remember when he was born," we went on, clichés spilling helplessly out of our mouths, embarrassing us all—why couldn't we just think them? why did we have to actually say them?—in exactly the same despised tone our maiden aunts had used accosting us on our birthdays. "Weren't we just at his *brith*? It seems like yesterday."

"What about the *brith?*" my grandmother and mother asked each other—and me—as Ben lay under the fluorescent lights in the hospital, waiting for his liver to kick into gear and clear his blood of its sludgy bilirubin. "It has to be on the eighth day," my grandmother insisted.

"They'll make allowances," I said. When to schedule the ritual circumcision was the last thing on my mind. Let the tradition fit the baby, not the other way around. In the days immediately after Ben's birth I was much more involved with doctors than rabbis. Let my father call the *mohel*—the rabbi specializing in circumcisions—order the food, make the phone calls. I didn't want to do anything but show up.

Yet not to have a *brith* never entered my mind, even after my medical school friends explained that it wasn't medically justifiable. "We can circumcise him here," Max had told me on the day we showed up at the hospital to take Ben home, "one, two, three." I declined. The point wasn't to get it over quickly, but to have the full-fledged ceremony.

Though I couldn't articulate it at the time, Ben's *brith* was important to me because it was vicariously mine: thirty years after the fact of my birth, I was ready to claim what had been ignobly withheld from me because of the accident of my gender. The birth of girls had always been surrounded by an absence of ritual: "naming ceremonies" for girls were of such recent vintage that everyone in my generation had missed out. A nice idea, I thought, bringing girl babies to synagogue to be formally named by a rabbi, but woefully inadequate as a compensatory gesture. How could the chanting of a few words begin to approximate the power of the ritual circumcision, the incising of flesh, the mandate for which comes from the Bible itself? Not until Ben's birth did I realize the degree to which I was an uninvited guest at my own religion, with its unrepentant sexism. Marginalized by a five-thousand-year-old tradition, I sought to claim my birthright through my son.

At the time, I let my parents shoulder the burden of planning the celebration. Though by rights David and I should have been the hosts, we counted ourselves among the grateful guests who gathered at my parents' house on a frigid Sunday morning in January. I had dressed Ben in a soft yellow dressing gown, the kind with a drawstring bottom—for easy access—a neighbor's hand-me-down that I loved for its soft, well-worn quality. Under the direction of the *mohel,* my father and I constructed a kind of dais for Ben, a platform out of pillows, blankets, and dishtowels. It rested on the card table that we'd placed in the den. During most family parties, the table functioned as a makeshift bar for the few bottles of liquor hardly anyone touched. Today the schnapps and Scotch were in the kitchen.

In a maternity dress, my breasts aching and leaking milk, feeling more female, more bovine, than I ever imagined possible, I stood at Ben's side. Only immediate family and a few close friends joined us; in the other rooms, the party swirled full swing, the food on the dining room table swathed in plastic, waiting to be opened, as after a funeral. It's not that for Jews life is a party, but rather that when so many people find themselves in the same house, you might as well eat.

My thoughts were far away. I was imagining a long, silent line of men, from Ben to David to our fathers to our grandfathers, a line snaking around the globe, across oceans and continents, the way movies indicate the advances of armies or the emigration of populations, ending in the desert, an unbroken string of Jewish men on whom this operation was performed in roughly the same way, for millennia. I didn't just see them; I almost heard them, a kind of shuffle, as if they were on a slow-paced but incessant march, as if they knew no rest. That baby on the blanketed platform was my father, my father-in-law, my husband's grandfather, their fathers at their side, these grandfathers as babies, and so on, an endless regression into the past. My son, with his dark hair, dark skin, belonged in that line.

Suddenly the *mohel* sprang into action. He directed my father to stand at Ben's head, David's father by his feet, and removed his instruments from an old-fashioned doctor's bag, talking all the while like the host of a late night talk show. This was man's work, though it looked like woman's. In fact, it looked, in all honesty, as if they were finicky cooks preparing a roast, choosing their utensils, debating degrees of sterility. Prayers began. The *mohel* dabbed the baby's mouth with some kind of alcohol, everyone jokey and loud as people tend to become when penises are under discussion or are exposed to plain air, while I kept up a soft patter to Ben, stroking his hand, his hair, as if he could hear me. A round metal instrument was applied to my son's penis. How icy it must feel on his impossibly soft flesh. I commanded myself to look even as he started to wail, a razor thin, piercing cry that increased in volume and pitch until a bud of blood appeared, and then he issued as curdling a scream as I'd ever heard. "He doesn't feel a thing," everyone told me, even the women, who should have known better.

Red faced with pain and shock and betrayal, Ben was

suddenly in my arms. He still had not inhaled. The men shook one another's hands, embraced, and repaired to the kitchen. They weren't drinkers, but God knew they needed one now.

In the rest of the house, for the shank of the day, the party continued—people ate, drank, talked, ate again. But I sat with my son in my girlhood bedroom, rocking him, nursing him, wondering if he'd ever stop crying, not blaming him if he wouldn't, if he'd ever forgive me for mutilating him. For that's what I'd done: I'd branded him.

Baptisms, immersions, christenings, *brith*s, all these ceremonies are performed when the child is as soft and warm, as fragrant and kneadable, as a loaf from the oven, before they have a chance to object in any way, to be cognizant. The incising of marks, the drawing of blood, altering of the flesh. I remembered the story of Abraham and Isaac, which I'd never understood. How could a father march a son up the mountain to certain sacrifice? Yet I had done the same thing because of a tradition I couldn't see, describe, or explain.

Twelve years later, I knew with the same unexamined, automatic certainty that I wanted to have a Bar Mitzvah for my son. Yet true to my family tradition, according to which religion was felt most strongly as a negation rather than an affirmation—don't drive on Shabbos, don't mix meat and dairy, don't even think about telling a lie—I knew only what kind I didn't want. Not to be countenanced was an indoor, cookie-cutter affair like everyone else's. Of all the scores of Bar and Bat Mitzvahs I'd attended, none was memorable; not one stood out in my mind.

"Oh, Bar Mitzvahs," said a neighbor. "You people get crazy. They're so garish, so glitzy. I heard about one where not only did they have valet parking at the country club, but the man who parked your car met you with a glass of champagne and a corsage for the woman—"

I cut her off. "Some people have that kind of Bar Mitzvah," I said, summoning all my self-righteousness, "and some people don't." In my mind I'd already convicted her of the worst kind of anti-Semitism.

Yet truthfully I couldn't think of one Bar Mitzvah that seemed tasteful to me, that I could have used as a model for the one I had in mind.

I wanted it to be an open-air party. If only our backyard were bigger. When we'd first moved to our house the two lots behind us were vacant, and our elderly neighbor would surely have let us pitch a tent, bring in some tables and chairs. But now two houses stood in what had once been our private park, and our own nicely landscaped but minuscule lot wasn't even large enough to accommodate a game of bad-minton.

Were there palatial houses on the water's edge we could rent, conference centers with rambling, manicured lawns, grand old hotels? Wasn't there somewhere a country club with a simple white house, good food, and a pretty view? But I knew that neither the festooned windows of country clubs nor the pine of a country inn would feel homey enough for me. Rather, it would feel as if we had moved into a furnished room and had to endure someone else's taste.

Anyway, I couldn't face having to deal with the personnel in catering halls. David and I had scouted a few country clubs before our wedding, where we were advised by men in expensive suits that we were the kind of people for whom less is more.

No, the Bar Mitzvah had to remain out of the hands of professional handlers and take place outdoors—this was nonnegotiable. Better to have the trees, sky, breeze; to be in a setting in which our size and stature weren't aggrandized, but quite the opposite. The celebration of a rite of passage, a change of state, demanded that we feel close to the earth and weather, not cocooned within a curtained room awash in re-cycled air.

"If you have it in a tent," my mother-in-law warned, "you won't be able to invite half the people you need to." This was the problem we'd had with our wedding.

"Let's make up a preliminary guest list," I told David one night before bed. I'd sketched out at least three, but I'd never consulted him—would he want to invite people from work? Distant cousins?

"Just invite the same people we invited to our wedding," he said.

"That was sixteen years ago," I reminded him. He shrugged and started naming names; I jotted them down. Without even thinking we drew up a list of seventy-five people.

"That's not so bad," he said.

"I can't believe how many people you left out," I began. "What about . . ." and I named at least twenty more people in as many seconds.

"Oh yeah," he said. "Right."

"But that makes about a hundred and twenty people," I moaned, "not including Ben's or our parents' friends. Now what?" I felt like wringing my hands. "Why are you smiling?"

"I can't believe we have so many friends."

He went to sleep, but I stayed up. Ellen, my oldest friend, from seventh grade, headed the list of guests. Next came Vicki Lens, my newest friend. There were people from every stratum of my life—from every school I'd ever attended, every job I'd ever held—from cities up and down the East Coast and across the country. This scrap of paper contained the archaeology of my life.

Though it was late and the house dark, I went downstairs to find my wedding album. The shock of how young David and I looked struck me full force even though I thought I'd prepared myself for it. Ben, I realized, was closer to the age we were when we married than David and I were now.

Who had chosen this album? I wondered, leafing through the pages. Who had selected this photo of me staring at a leaf, with one hand to my breast? Had I sleepwalked through my entire wedding?

When I reached the pictures of the tables of guests, I studied each page carefully: only five friends from our wedding were on my list of Bar Mitzvah invitees. There were some people whose names I couldn't remember, people I wouldn't know how to begin getting back in touch with, if I wanted to. What were they doing there?

But the larger question, I was realizing, was why I had had such a traditional Jewish wedding. Everything else about my betrothal had been informal. David hadn't sunk down on one knee; instead, our decision had evolved, slowly and organically, after a year of spending just about every day in each other's company.

At first, David suggested that we simply move in together.

But I was keen on getting married. "Help me understand why," David said. We'd both lived with other people, I tried to explain to him. The more completely I believed in something, it seemed, the less eloquently I could put it into words. Living together was like making camp: you staked out ground, put up your tent, laid out your sleeping bags, and stayed as long as you wanted.

The institution of marriage, however, existed apart from us. Like a serviceable, solid shelter you came upon while hiking in the woods, it spared you the trouble of making camp anew. And it was a pleasant place to spend the night, full of the smells and echoes of those who had used it before you, who had maybe left a tin cup, or a pot, or initials etched into a stone; when you mixed the embers in the neat but small fire ring lined with stones, their presence rose to your nostrils. Marriage was something we didn't have to create ourselves but would enter into, something that had endured through the ages, something we could partake of, something bigger than we were, that could comfort and contain us.

David understood, but our friends didn't: to them, we were pariahs, traitors. I couldn't make them understand. Neither could I make my parents, or David's, understand that despite our willingness to go public we still considered our relationship intensely personal and private. Our decision to devote our lives to each other intersected almost nowhere with family, with fortunes, contracts, or caterers. Don't buy me silver or register me for china patterns, I told my mother and prospective mother-in-law, who acquiesced but secretly thought I was out of my mind. Our marriage wasn't about acquiring, about setting up house, about pragmatic matters. If we were going to get married, it would be within a context we ourselves defined.

"We want you to come to dinner at our house with David's parents," I told my parents during a Sunday lunch at their house.

"That's not how it's done," my mother said. "We'll invite them to our house first."

How *what* was done? I wanted to ask her. What I was talking about had no relation to anyone else's wedding. Just because I decided to marry didn't mean I was embracing convention in all its stultifying incarnations.

"We want to be married outdoors," we told our parents.

"A catering hall is more practical," my future in-laws said.

"The food has to be kosher," my parents said. "There has to be a *chuppah,* and you have to wear a veil."

No to the catering hall, yes to kosher, to the *chuppah,* even, at the last moment, to the veil—why fight about it? The only detail that didn't come up for negotiation was who would officiate at the service. A rabbi, of course, my father's rabbi. No question. And yes, we'd even consent to having a prenuptial talk with him.

"Take your ring off," I instructed David as we waited for the rabbi to open his office door that August afternoon. We'd bought our wedding bands the day before at a jewelry store in the Village—three interlocking bands in pink, white, and yellow gold: the self, the other, us. The rabbi's study was dark and cool, the walls book lined. He wore a dark suit, his signature gold pinky ring, and a huge smile. "I don't need to tell you what an asset your father is to this shul," he said, and I nodded. "We wanted him to become president," he continued. "But your father refused. I never understood why."

I hadn't known of the offer, but my father's refusal didn't surprise me. Dig deep enough into my family's commitment to religion and you'd hit the bedrock of negation.

"Do you have your wedding ring?" the rabbi asked me. "Tradition calls for a plain gold band," he mused, playing with mine. I showed him how, if you dropped it on the desk, it assumed its proper configuration, the bands crisscrossing each other like a snake settling down for a nap. He tried it and smiled, like a magician with a new trick. "Very mystical," he said. "Judaism has a rich mystical tradition." The ring made a tiny tinkling sound, and I thought of the keys on my old toy piano.

"Well, I think it will do," he said, handing it back. "Do you have any special requests for the ceremony?" We discussed my desire that he proclaim us "husband and wife" and that he strike "obey" from the vows. I asked if he could read a special passage from the Song of Songs that made reference to mourning doves, in memory of David's sister, who had died just a few months earlier.

"No special vows? You're not going to write your own?" No, we both told him, the traditional vows were fine for us. This was no hippie marriage on a mountaintop.

I waited for him to talk about the sanctity of marriage, its sacredness. Maybe he expected that my parents had already done that; maybe he was being realistic. I half expected him to ask me about the *mikvah,* about whether I knew the laws of family purity, which dictate when a married couple can have relations. But he didn't say a word.

Shaking hands good-bye, he told me again what a pillar of the synagogue my father was. I thanked him and summoned the image of my father rising from his chair, gathering his books, sighing with fatigue and burdened by conflicting loyalties, to head out into the night and the synagogue. Of my mother's baleful look, as if he were heading out to his bookie's to bet on the horses. Of how she was always in bed, asleep, when he came home.

Just because I couldn't eat a thing the entire day of my

wedding didn't mean that I was nervous. I wasn't. The ceremony took place in the shadiest recess of my parents' next-door neighbors' yard. The ground was soft and wet under our feet. The day before, a thunderstorm had threatened to unmoor the tent pilings. But Sunday had dawned clear and fresh, if a little windy. The *chuppah* looked like a bedsheet drying in the sun; my favorite uncle held one pole, my childhood boyfriend another. Standing under it, I remembered the *succah* my grandmother had once taken me to in the backyard of the Queens storefront shul. It was during the harvest holiday of Succoth, when religious Jews eat all their meals for eight days in small wooden booths that they build and decorate. The earth was spongy and the shade almost dank. Fruit and vegetables hung from the ceiling.

Fruit was in the passage from the Song of Songs that the rabbi read at our request. A breeze rustled the trees above us—my sister-in-law's spirit, I knew. My grandmother's diamond engagement ring, which my grandfather had bought in 1925 for $125, flashed on my finger when I held the cup of wine for David to drink.

We said our vows, exchanged rings, and then the rabbi, his fingers forming a tent over our heads, the same tent my grandmothers drew with their hands lighting Shabbos candles, began the blessing, "May the countenance of the Lord bless you and keep you. May the Lord show you favor, and be gracious unto you. May the Lord show you kindness and grant you peace. Amen." Ancient words that whispered of time itself, which had been intoned over countless couples standing as we did, facing east to Jerusalem, in Hebrew and in English. For the first time all day I felt myself close to weeping. This was all we had, the best we could do, to come together this way, to cleave unto one another, to create a clearing in the wilderness.

I remember the high shine on David's black shoes as he stepped on the glass to shatter it, to remind us that in happiness comes sadness, the sight of Ellen sitting in the front row, dabbing her eyes, and the tender way David cupped my face in his hands to kiss me, as if he'd never before touched me.

David and I drove home that night, as we had countless times before, on the Long Island Expressway, the Grand Central, across the Triborough Bridge, down 125th Street; we found a parking space, tucked as many presents as we could under our arms—silver trays, china vases, toaster ovens—and rang for the elevator.

"You guys pull off a heist?" asked one of our neighbors, a single man on the third floor.

"We just got married," David said.

"Well, congratulations," he said, holding the door for us. Our apartment was waiting, small and dark, offering us a perfect view of several nearby water towers.

"Feel any different?" I asked David before we went to sleep.

"Not yet."

I didn't, either.

"Glad it's over?" he asked.

"Yeah," I said, meaning it. But also sad. The day had been a blur of faces, high feeling, good jazz, people arriving and leaving, and now it was past. On my wedding night I realized I was a virgin—not in terms of sex, but ritual. My marriage, at age twenty-five, was the first ceremony in which I'd been a celebrant, the first religious ritual in which I'd participated.

I'd been unprepared for the solemnity underlying the gaiety, the way walking on a country lane you hear a rushing stream though you can't see water, except for an occasional trickle, and realize finally that the water is running beneath your feet, beneath the road, accompanying your every step; that in all probability the road was built to hug the stream, that the stream engineered the most efficient way from here to there.

"You won't believe this," my friend Joan told me barely a half moment after we kissed each other hello. We were having dinner together in a local diner. Once upon a time, when our lives were an easier brew of work and domestic responsibilities, we met monthly, ordered drinks, sat back, and let the lazy stream of our conversation meander wherever it wanted. These days we found ourselves preparing for our semiannual get-togethers as if they were oral examinations, compressing all the headlines and highlights of the past six months—what had happened with friends, family, work—into a taut, highly structured, purposeful presentation. Lost were not only the tasty details, but the luxurious ease, the heightened anticipation, with which you approach a meal at a three-star restaurant.

"The strangest thing has happened," she continued, getting right to the point, speaking softly, half covering her mouth with her cupped hand, as if she were about to confess something lurid. "You know how much I've always resisted going to church, how I made my husband take the kids to religion—if he wanted to have them confirmed, it was his job to get them to Sunday school. . . . Well, about two months ago, I heard about this church in the next town. It's right on the water, and people, friends of mine, were raving about it—the pastor's sermons, the music, the setting, it was all fabulous, and I had to see it. To make a long story short, we went there for mass one Sunday, and now—this is so weird—the kids are enrolled in Sunday school, we go to mass almost every week, and I'm on three committees."

"St. Mary's, right?" I said, interrupting her.

She was amazed. "How do you know?"

"I've been hearing about this church for months," I told her. One by one, many of my Catholic friends had defected from their parish churches for St. Mary's—which they all described as homier, more inviting, and more welcoming.

To the waitress hovering in the corner, waiting for the right moment to come and take our order, we must have looked as if we were confessing our most recent affairs, as if we were trading stories of furtive glances, stolen kisses, illicit trysts.

"Anyway," I continued, "you won't believe this, but the same thing has happened to me."

"You?" She was shocked.

"I mean, we joined the synagogue over a year ago, I told you, but I just joined my first committee. Social Action."

"That's the one I joined," she said. We looked at each other with amazement. Even in the midst of this unexpected and surprising complicity we both felt faintly embarrassed, and unsure why. It was almost as if we'd been bracing ourselves for the response we felt sure we'd get—a sarcastic, eye-rolling, "Oh no, don't tell me you've found religion at this late date"—only to feel disarmed by our startling synchronicity.

We took a sip of beer and pondered our embarrassment. It had something to do with the feeling that something from our deep past had surfaced, something we'd put years of energy into suppressing, even denying—as if an acquaintance we'd banished from our lives had turned up on the doorstep long after we'd forgotten about him. Religion? Churchgoing? These were issues we hadn't discussed publicly for years, since high school.

"We don't go to services regularly or anything," I said hastily. "I mean, I'm mostly in it for the camaraderie. And so that Ben can go to Hebrew school."

"Sure," Joan chimed in. "I mean, we go on Sundays, but not every Sunday. And it's mostly for the kids. And so that I can feel as if I'm taking part in some kind of social and political action."

"Yes, that's very important to me, too," I told her solemnly. "The most important part. I keep telling myself, my involvement is about everything but God."

"Exactly," she said.

We were kidding ourselves. But we didn't yet have the vocabulary, much less the confidence, to talk about what was really happening to us. What we were really stumbling over was the discovery that after our formal rejection of organized religion twenty-five years ago, we were in fact still Jews, or Catholics, or Baptists at heart. That we bore the stamp of our ancestors, our parents. That the legacy we'd spent years avoiding or denying surfaced despite our efforts—the way Yiddish words bubbled up unbidden in my inner dialogue or an old stain appeared on a couch after years of use. That there was something comforting about clannishness, about the tribal mentality we'd spent years noisily eschewing. That we wanted to find ways to imbue our children with these feelings without feeling hypocritical. And that we could find a way to take charge of our religious life while at the same time admitting to what John Updike called the "humiliation of belief." Or at least of belonging.

But I think we were both secretly amazed that they let us come, they let us sit in services, even though we weren't sure about anything. There was no entrance exam, no prerequisites, you didn't have to swear to anything; you just, apparently, showed up, and after that you could do as much or as little as you wanted.

We didn't trust this open admissions policy. What we didn't know how to say was that we weren't definitive about the state of our belief in God. We felt as if we had a spiritual life, but whether God was at the center of it we weren't sure. Shouldn't that have disqualified us? We were waiting for the sniffing dogs, the Geiger counter, the metal detector, to weed us out.

May 1994: "Hello, Roberta, this is Ron Friedman from Kehillath Shalom"—another perfect stranger. Why did everyone who called from this congregation sound so hearty on
the phone, as if we knew each other, or at least had good
friends in common? Like Eve Lodge, he didn't presume intimacy, only interest, good fellowship. "I'm calling as the chair
of the Nominating Committee. Carol Rubin"—the president
of the congregation—"would very much like it if you'd agree
to serve on the committee with us. We're charged with coming up with a slate of officers for elections this June. She
thought you'd be a wonderful addition."

I was so nonplussed that I didn't utter my usual, reflexive, "No, sorry, I can't." The request was more than preposterous—it was gratuitous. Carol Rubin didn't know me;
we'd never once spoken. I'd only admired her from afar, the
type of woman, slightly older than I, whom I could only hope
to emulate, who looked, despite her gray hair, as if she still
had miles and miles in front of her, who could speak with
both passion and firmness. I was hugely flattered that she'd
thought of me, and completely bewildered. What could I
possibly contribute to this committee? I didn't know anyone
in the congregation. How could I possibly decide whom to
nominate?

"Vicki is on the committee as well," Ron continued, and went on to cite a few other names, none familiar to me.

"I'll have to think about it," I said.

"That's fine," Ron said, sounding grateful for anything short of outright rejection. He explained that the committee would have to meet several times within the next few weeks, but that we'd disband as soon as we made our recommendations.

"It will mean several nights out," I told David.

"Do it if you want," he said. So I did.

"I have a meeting tonight," I said during dinner.

"Again?" whined Jacob, crestfallen, as if I left him alone every night.

"You're always going out," Ben said petulantly, studying his food.

"It just seems that way," I explained. The Nominating Committee had met twice the previous week and again tonight. I had yet to attend a religious service and had little desire to do so, yet these committees drew me out of my house, overcame my inertia, and I wasn't sure why. I liked getting together with like-minded people to watch them work. I enjoyed seeing people's personalities emerge, enjoyed listening. Everyone was intelligent and good-hearted;

we were all there because we felt it was important to take time away from our kids, our spouses, our own pursuits in order to—what, exactly? To make sure that this organization kept on working, retained its place in the community of Huntington, its tiny hold on the world; that it stayed in existence, remained afloat. It was a kind of altruism in action I hadn't experienced in years.

Yet I was still more observer than participant. Even though I drove to the first Nominating Committee meeting with Vicki, with whom I was quickly becoming a friend, I felt alone once we arrived: she knew everyone, I knew only a few others. We sat around a table, sipping tea, munching cookies, talking about people whose names sounded familiar but whose faces I couldn't picture. What in the world am I doing here? I wondered to myself. I felt embarrassed that I had nothing to contribute. Yet no one seemed to expect anything from me, short of not falling asleep at the table. I was benignly ignored.

The process of nomination entailed spinning through a mental Rolodex of membership and trying to come up with the name of anyone who might be arm-twisted into serving as either an officer or a trustee of the synagogue. Back and forth across the table names flew, like cards being dealt at a high-stakes poker game—she'll agree to a trusteeship, but not vice presidency; he'll be vice president, but only if she's on the board. Phone calls were made, names were added, scratched off, put back in. How few congregants I actually knew, how tiny my involvement, how tenuous my hold or understanding of what was happening.

Yet I felt oddly comfortable when I looked around the table, though many were complete strangers, and some much older than I was. My children were in elementary school; Ron's son was in high school; Jerry's children were married and probably had children of their own. These older members were either founding members—the synagogue began in 1969 as a place where politics and social justice would be wedded to liturgy and prayer—or had joined out of principle. Many families my age were here by default, because this was the least objectionable synagogue we could imagine. Yet this largely negative attraction had spawned a positive one, at least for Vicki and me. Against all odds, against the backdrop of wildly divergent lives and priorities, we sat together, pulling for the common good, trying to come up with the name of just one individual who would make the sacrifice to become president, vice president, to lead us for the next two years. Many of these folks, I realized slowly, had been coming together this way for years and years, moving on and off the board, editing the newsletter, chairing key committees. I hadn't served on a governing board since ninth grade, when, having lost a close race for school treasurer, I accepted a post as chair of the elections committee.

"Recording secretary," Ron was saying when I returned to the conversation, scratching his head with the eraser end of his pencil. "Sharon doesn't want to do that anymore."

"What's involved?" I asked.

"Coming to board meetings and taking minutes."

"I can do that," I heard myself say.

Everyone turned to look at me.

"I'm a writer," I said.

Eagerly they wrote my name down, before I could change my mind.

As the meeting broke up, I took my time leaving, trying to look busy while I waited for Vicki to finish chatting with everyone. An older woman approached me and stuck out her hand. "I'm Harriet," she said. "I'm very pleased to meet you, and look forward to seeing you at the board meetings. You'll do just fine."

"I can't believe I got myself into this," I told Vicki on the drive home, thinking of all the complications, my children's reactions, to say nothing of David's, the weight of one more responsibility. I knew Joan would smile when she heard.

"It'll be fun," Vicki said. "We'll drive to meetings together."

"Hebrew school's on Tuesdays," I reminded her. That meant two trips to the synagogue, a few hours apart. We'd personally be responsible for wearing a groove in Roller Coaster Road.

What I didn't tell her was that I loved the drive, that it had become, in a curious way, the place where I felt most connected to my father. I didn't hear his voice, or talk to him, as I sometimes did when I was puttering around the house; I simply felt his presence in the car with me—perhaps because I always tried to calculate how many miles he had driven me around Long Island when I was a teenager.

Immediately after his death, he'd seemed simply gone, vanished, as if the heat of that blistering July Fourth weekend when he died had evaporated every trace of him. On the short ride from my parents'—now my mother's—house to the funeral chapel, the limousine stopped to let a family of ducks cross the road. I told Ben, nestled between my husband and me, to look at the ducks. But he burrowed his head into my shoulder. He didn't want to be told to look at anything, afraid of what he'd find. I didn't blame him.

"But what happens to Papa Jack's body?" he'd asked again, as he had earlier, at breakfast. Apparently, our previous answer hadn't satisfied him. I wondered if he'd heard anything we'd told him, about his grandpa's illness. He'd hardly asked any questions during the year it had taken for us to realize that my father's cancer hadn't been arrested by an operation and chemotherapy, but had spread. Now, with my mother sitting across from us, too numb to cry, and too many others in earshot, he asked again.

"It goes back to the earth," I said. And then I simply tuned out. My husband would have to supply the specifics.

I'd also been spared selecting the coffin; my mother and my father's closest friend had seen to that. There it sat, draped with an Israeli flag, in the corner of the room where we all met, kissed, shook hands, and gave one another sorrowful looks, before being shown into the chapel. "The Lord is my Shepherd," the rabbi intoned, and I recalled Mrs. Marsh, a sixth-grade teacher from my Queens elementary school who recited the psalm each Friday morning during assembly, for which girls had to wear white shirts and blue neckerchiefs, the boys white shirts and ties.

The funeral itself seemed like a school assembly. We stood up, we sat down; my grandmother fainted and revived; prayers were read. Then I walked up to the podium and read a brief eulogy I'd composed the night before on my mother's old manual typewriter, grateful for the task, for the momentary diversion:

> On special Saturday afternoons years ago, my father
> would take us to the place where he worked, a huge
> factory with rows of shelves, cartons, and imposing-
> looking equipment. His was not a desk job—too often
> his attention was needed in different parts of the

building—but he had a desk and I loved to sit in his chair and snoop around. One day I opened his top drawer and found to my amazement a pair of tortoiseshell eyeglasses. It was stunning, this discovery that at work he was a different person, a person who wore glasses, something he never did when he was busy being my father. It was as if I'd stumbled upon his secret identity.

But my father had no secret identity. In fact, he was, as my husband said yesterday, one of the most consistent men he'd ever known. My father presented one face to the world—a face filled with strength, generosity, courage, and love for his family, a love so strong it was almost palpable. . . .

My in-laws watched over my son during the service, and at the cemetery, where the sun glanced off the stones as blindingly as it did at the beach. I remember looking at my mother's collar, where that morning she'd painstakingly snipped a bright red bow from her otherwise somber navy blue dress, working at it with her old nail scissors, the same ones with which my father used to cut my finger- and toenails when I was a girl. I lingered to throw some dirt on the grave. "Grant eternal life, O God," the rabbi intoned.

The Jewish religion is an understanding but strong-armed parent to mourners. Grief, it knows, is a condition one must be gently but firmly weaned of. First you get the body in the ground, as quickly and as simply as possible, since there's no point delaying the inevitable. Then you go back home, wash your hands, eat an egg, and open your front door and sit—in the old days, on hard boxes—while neighbors and friends swarm over, your house a temporary hive. For seven days you sit like a queen on her minimalist throne. The rabbi and congregation members come to you to say prayers for the dead, the peculiar Jewish Kaddish, which never mentions death or sorrow, only praise for God, and neighbors bring platters of food. On the seventh day you walk around the block to signify your reentry into the world. ("Remember when Daddy planted these curb trees?" my mother asked me as we circled her street. "They were tiny spindly things; no one thought they'd survive the winter." Now they were tall, full-bodied trees, their roots slanting the sidewalk slabs into strange acute angles, as if a tiny earthquake had taken place.)

This walk inaugurates a thirty-day period of still intense but not primary mourning. You begin to go to services daily to say Kaddish and continue for ten more months. ("I never realized how comforting it was to go to shul," my mother told me the next June, "until the eleven months were over.") You keep socializing to a minimum. Wear subdued colors. Don't go to movies.

I observed none of this. I'd grieve on my own, my own way. And I began by leaving my mother that morning of the seventh day—at her insistence, though it was one of the hardest partings I've ever endured—to drive back up to the country house, where I'd learned, from a midnight telephone call a scant week ago, of my father's death.

I found myself reluctant to return to our downstairs bedroom, where I'd taken the call; I made David walk with me, as if I were convalescent. And I slept badly that first night. In the morning, before anyone was up, I dressed and walked down to the lake.

It was a misty morning, the sun lost behind a wax-paper screen. The sky looked more immense than I'd ever noticed. I felt more than bereft, I felt exposed, as if the ozone layer over me had evaporated, had left me in mortality's glare. My legs grew weak; I wanted to get down on the ground, feel its support beneath me—a melodramatic, nearly histrionic gesture, but one that felt true, genuinely right. How could I go on, I wailed, how could I raise my sons, how could I buy a house, how could I navigate this world without my father's guidance?

Through my tears, I found myself remembering a dream I'd had the night before. I had boarded a ferry teeming with passengers resembling refugees bound for Liberty Island, the island on which the Statue of Liberty stands—no great coincidence there: my father had died on Independence Day. Yet the boat headed east toward the open Atlantic, not west toward New Jersey. Even more confusing and upsetting, I'd been separated from the friends with whom I was traveling. But just then, in the distance loomed an island no one had ever seen before, an island bathed in a shimmering Mediterranean light, a golden island, in perpetual sunshine. "That's the New Jordan," people began whispering, crying with astonishment and joy, "the New Jordan."

It was as nearly a dream of paradise as I'd ever had, yet I felt terribly distressed, and not a little guilty, recalling it. How could I have had this utopian dream, this dream of liberation, so soon after my father's death? Clearly the events were related, but in ways I didn't wish to explore.

"It's your father's final gift to you," said a friend who had lost her father a few years earlier. "Your vision of the island is what your father wished he could give you but couldn't, everything he wanted you to have but was blocked from offering, for so many complicated reasons. You are free now— free to get there, to take what you want."

Yes. I believed my friend's interpretation before I understood or accepted it. Every experience, a college Shakespeare professor had taught me, contains its opposite: within every loss lies the kernel of a gain. Though my father couldn't have been more generous—with his time, his love, his devotion to me—he nevertheless couldn't give me everything I wanted from him.

I kept these complicated, contradictory thoughts with me, the way I would an heirloom he'd bequeathed to me, and slowly, over the years, I felt my father being restored to me. This is not to say that I didn't live through days when I missed him beyond words, when I cried as if my grief were raw.

But since the dream about the New Jordan I couldn't shake the sense that my father was within me, almost as if he'd been transformed into a tiny homunculus who now resided in some remote part of my body, as if I were pregnant with him, never to give birth. I couldn't explain the certainty with which I believed in his continued existence, but nonetheless I did. What an irony. In life, my father, the most rational of men, taught me all I knew about using my intellect to its best advantage; through his death he taught me rationality's opposite: to divorce understanding from belief, to be certain of things I couldn't explain, to take comfort from sources I couldn't identify—to believe.

In January David and I received an unexpected invitation to the Bar Mitzvah of the son of one of my distant cousins. "We have to go," I told David; what a perfect opportunity to watch from a distance, to gather data like spies on a reconnaissance mission.

We had to get up early Saturday in order to dress and deposit the boys at my in-laws. Slipping into fancy clothes and makeup at eight-thirty in the morning made us feel as if we had jet lag.

The synagogue was very grand, boasting a balcony and upholstered pews. David and I sat near the back, open prayer books in our laps, yet we scarcely looked at them. Our eyes were everywhere, trying to drink in all the details, down to the color of the yarmulkes, the position of the flowers on the *bimah.* Each synagogue's morning service was as unique as a thumbprint, a seamless amalgam of personality, tradition, and the desire to tamper with tradition. We'd seen cantors break out guitars and produce tambourines from beneath their flowing robes; we'd heard rabbis thunder from the pulpit like prophets, and others whisper so softly to the Bar Mitzvah boy that you felt as if you were eavesdropping. This ceremony added a lovely touch: with the Bar Mitzvah boy and his family gathered on the *bimah,* the Torah, the repository of Jewish learning, the core of Judaism, the sacred book from which all else flowed, was passed from rabbi to grandparents to parents to son, a literal enactment of the fact that by Bar Mitzvah age a boy is ready to assume the responsibilities of a Jewish man. It's a weighty tome, the Torah, two scrolls written on parchment, dressed in velvet covers with silver crowns and adornments, and when he received it the boy grimaced, as if he didn't expect such weight.

This hand-to-hand transmission of the Torah was the beating heart of Judaism, the physical rendering of the scriptural imperative to entrust our children with that which had once been entrusted to us. Itself, the book was nothing more than a community diary, a collection of stories of a rambunctious Semitic tribe that defiantly created meaning out of a moral wilderness and clung to it, conceived of one God out of a multitude, and insisted against all odds that life be lived as if it had a purpose—and it, in turn, gave meaning to life. Those aspects of the chronicle that excluded me I could reconstruct to include me; I could insist on my inclusion as stubbornly as my ancestors clung to their iconoclastic beliefs. I was there at Sinai; and there was still room for me in the synagogue of American Judaism, even if I had to carve out the niche myself. But in fact I wasn't alone.

"Why do you think the ceremonies are all so different," I asked my husband as we drove from the synagogue to the country club for the reception, "and yet the parties are all the same?"

Sure enough, the afternoon party was a replay of thousands of others. Just enough food was served during cocktails to make you say, "I couldn't possibly eat another thing," and then it was time for the main meal. Dancing teenagers, dressed as if they'd shopped in a little boutique on Pluto, ushered us into the main dining room, where a DJ was already working the mike, controlling the pace and decibel level of the party. As if we were guests for a talk show taping, we were exhorted to stand, applaud, stamp our feet, and welcome our guests; then to swivel our hips, get down, boogie till the cows came home. But first—a set of "traditional" Jewish music—an electronic hora during which snaking circles were formed, hands were clapped, chairs with our hosts hoisted into the air. "Ach, what a party," everyone said, wiping their brows, returning to their seats, trying to avoid the waiters taking our orders, serving our food, more than three-quarters of which went back to the kitchen, untouched, and into the trash.

Four hours later David and I stumbled into our car, slipped the valet a few bucks, and sat in silence. Stuffed from eating too much, tired from smiling too much as we kept up a conversation with people we knew only glancingly, deaf from listening to music at too loud a volume, we looked at each other and shook our heads.

"Why don't we scrap the whole party idea and take a family trip?" I asked. Ellen's family had gone to Israel on the occasion of her younger brother's Bar Mitzvah, and it always struck me as a superior idea. Rather than spending money on throwaway party favors and an easily forgotten meal, we could travel, show the boys a part of the world they'd never seen, something they'd remember forever. Israel was the obvious choice. But we could also go out west. . . .

"Because Ben doesn't want to take a trip. He wants a party." This was true. Ben didn't have much experience with Bar Mitzvahs, but since everyone else in his Hebrew school class was having a traditional celebration, he wanted one, too.

"And what do you want?"

"I want us to have a simple outdoor party. We'll find a way."

"What's that?" Ben asked sullenly one Sunday morning as we walked up the rickety steps of the synagogue to Hebrew school.

"Looks like a tent," I said. In the yard adjoining the building. Of course. Why didn't I think of it? We could pitch a tent right here. That would make things so easy. Home away from home. Exactly what I always wanted.

# CHAPTER 4

# Inclusion/ Exclusion

"re you Jewish?" I ask the boy sitting across from me. I don't think he is, though I'm not sure why. What makes someone one religion and not another? Most of my friends are Jewish, but some are Christians. They can drive every day of the week and eat whatever they want—there's nothing they can't do. Each spring, Christian girls my age dress up like brides in miniature white bridal gowns, veils, and trains, white Mary Janes, and carry bouquets of flowers to and from church. They pose for photographs in the park across from our house. I can't stop watching them.

Suddenly my teacher, my beloved Mrs. Bentley, stops writing at her desk and turns her attention entirely to me.

"We don't ask anyone about their religion," she says, frowning, barely able to contain her displeasure and disappointment. All year I'd been a good student—kept my desk neat, paid attention. I didn't even cry the first day of school. But now she's furious at me, and I don't know why.

"That's private," she says, and even though I don't understand what she means, she doesn't say another word. John looks at me impassively. He has soft, blotchy freckles all over his face, and he always wears a sweater vest, a shirt with buttons, and a little bow tie. He's definitely not Jewish.

I bet he goes to the Roman Catholic church across from the public library, on the corner of Bell Boulevard and 73rd Avenue, the end of our apartment development neighborhood and the beginning of the next, the one with private houses. I'm allowed to walk to the library by myself after school, and sometimes I think of crossing the street and stepping into the church. It has tan brick on the outside and a big stained-glass window. I imagine it's dark and quiet inside, but I'm not sure.

Lizzie and Marie go to that church, but only when their grandmother comes from France to visit. She's their father's mother, and she wears a huge cross around her neck. Their mother is Jewish. She never goes to synagogue, not even on the High Holy Days. Though we play with Lizzie and Marie almost every day, we make a special visit to their apartment in

December, just before Christmas, to admire their tree and all their carefully wrapped presents. Colored electric lights, glistening pine needles—these are outdoor things that don't belong inside. They also have a candle holder that looks just like a menorah but isn't. It has the wrong number of candles.

"What's the difference between Catholic and Christian?" I ask my mother over and over. I can never remember which group is bigger and which is smaller. But it really doesn't matter. There are more Jews than anything else.

Congenitally early, typically anxious, I walked into the synagogue on the first Tuesday evening of September 1994 in my new capacity as recording secretary to the board of trustees—and gasped. I'd heard rumors that the old building was to be renovated, and a computer-printed sign stating "Pardon our appearance, we're reconstructing" had been tacked to the front door for months. Yet nothing prepared me for what I saw when I walked inside.

The dingy, jerry-built sanctuary was—gone. In fact, much of the back half of the old building had been demolished. What would eventually take its place existed only in the crudest form, just a step or two away from the blueprint—without Sheetrock, only exposed beams, joists, and studs hinted of the room that would be created. I could discern the vague shape of vaulted ceiling and a cupola, and frames for twelve plain windows, asymmetrically placed on the wall facing the treed hillside.

"Awesome, isn't it?"

I looked toward the voice. The president of the board, a man who reminded me of my father, emerged out of a dark corner, carrying a door. Together we placed it on a couple of sawhorses that we positioned under a bare light bulb suspended from the ceiling, swept nails and debris from the plywood floor, gathered a few metal folding chairs strewn around the room, and established some semblance of a table around which to conduct a meeting.

The room was redolent of sawdust and reminded me of my father's basement workroom, where all his woodworking plans took shape, a place of infinite possibilities. I milled about aimlessly, poking into corners, steering clear of electrical wires. The space had the feel of a barn pressed into service as a summer stock theater, a place where the line between indoor and outdoor was effectively blurred. The other board members began arriving one by one, gasping as they entered. They seemed like actors in a postmodern play, trying to find their marks on the floor, unsure whether the play had already begun.

Religion began as theater, I recalled as I scrambled during the meeting to remember people's names, take notes, and pay attention to all the issues being debated back and forth. In ancient times the itinerant tribes of Israel took their holy ark with them as they traveled from one watering spot to the next and would erect a platform or stage on which to offer animal sacrifices. Yet every road show needed support staff to make sure that people and animals were fed, to drum up an audience. That's how the board of trustees appeared to me that night; we were a production company, responsible for ensuring that the show would go on.

To look around the table and realize how many people I knew, if only by sight, and to see the several people with whom David and I were quickly becoming friends was to see how deeply we'd become woven into the social fabric of the synagogue in only a year. Strangely enough, I felt as if I knew even the people I didn't know, though the source of this familiarity wasn't clear.

About the same time I'd begun attending the Social Action Committee meetings, I'd also joined a community chorus. Not only was I one of the youngest members by at least a couple of decades, but I also realized, after few rehearsals, that I was probably the only Jew. And though my sister sopranos were friendly, and chatted with me between songs, I hadn't made a single real friend. Conversations with them were stunted. I interrupted, responded too quickly, assumed meanings they didn't intend. Like books in a foreign language, I couldn't read them: I couldn't interpret, from their clothes, their hairdos, their pocketbooks, their carriage, who they were or what they did. They remained strangers; rather, I felt like a stranger—a sojourner, like Abraham, in their midst.

Around this board table, however, I felt as if I could speed-read everyone—the broad themes, if not the tiny details. I could tell who was from the Bronx and who from Brooklyn; I knew who had changed clothes before coming to the meeting and who hadn't. They were, as my grandmother would have said, using a term that had never failed to make me cringe, *landsmen,* people who were from the same country in which you were born. We spoke the same language, inflected our words with the same music, ate the same foods, shopped in the same stores, gave money to the same organizations.

That didn't mean we always agreed. One of the last items on the evening's agenda was whether or not to follow through on a member's suggestion and invite a gospel choir from a community church to perform in the synagogue. Suddenly sparks flew and tempers flared. While some of us found the prospect delightful—I was squarely in this camp, though I didn't speak up—the majority of the board members found the program very problematic.

"I don't want to hear songs glorifying Christ in our sanctuary," one man said. He, and others, had clearly been scarred by a brand of anti-Semitism to which I'd never been exposed—blatant, rampant, ugly—the kind that did damage to the way you think of yourself.

"You're part of the problem," someone responded. "We have to figure out ways of living together, of living in this community. If we shut our doors too tightly, we'll suffocate."

"If we let everyone in, we'll lose our identity."

Finally it came down to a vote that wasn't close—the invitation would not be proffered. I left the meeting disappointed but also with a new, sober understanding. The board did much more than allocate money and schedule events: it was the gatekeeper, responsible for deciding whom to let in, whom to keep out; who belongs and who is a stranger.

Negotiating borders is a question not only for the synagogue, but for every Jew, every member of a minority group. As individuals who exist in many communities at once, we feel like professional guests, acting differently depending on where we find ourselves—at home with our families; in a synagogue, with other Jews; in the supermarket or on the train, in society at large.

The last order of business that night dealt with preparations for the High Holy Days. With discussions of prayer books, donation cards, and ushers swirling around me, I realized that I too was facing a border I hadn't yet negotiated. I'd been to countless meetings by now, served on two committees, and here I sat taking notes, yet I hadn't once attended services. That door, for many reasons, was one I'd kept firmly shut.

"You know, I've been thinking," I told David. We'd just woken up to a sunny September morning, the first day of Rosh Hashanah, the Jewish New Year. "I think I'd like to go to services."

"Whatever," he said, and turned over to go back to sleep.

"No, I mean all of us. As a family."

He didn't answer at first. Then he sighed. "If you want," he said.

The boys were much less easily convinced. "Do we *have* to?" they asked a hundred times before breakfast.

"Yes," I said as firmly as I could muster. "You do." I wanted them to hear the blowing of the shofar, or ram's horn, the climax of the Rosh Hashanah service, summoning Jews to worship and repentance as it had in the desert generations ago.

The boys were grumpy and mind-splittingly slow. They dressed themselves in wholly inappropriate clothes—tattered jeans, sweatshirts. Only after intricate negotiations—yes, you can wear sneakers (actually, they had no other shoes); yes, you can call your friend to play the minute we get home; no, you can't wear your baseball cap—they were ready. Sulking, but ready.

Then I had about five minutes in which to shower, eat breakfast, scour my closet for a suitable dress, and dig up a pair of panty hose from the depths of my top dresser drawer. When I was a girl, I recalled, trying to find my black pumps in a too cluttered closet, Rosh Hashanah was the time to get a whole new outfit. Now, as I put on my grandmother's diamond engagement ring and my gold bracelet and diamond stud earrings, I envisioned my mother. The Jewish holidays were the one time a year that she allowed herself to wear her good jewelry, which was kept otherwise in the dark reaches of her chifforobe or the even darker recesses of the bank vault. "I don't want to show off," she'd explain—a vestigial response that made no sense to me, which in fact infuriated me, until I read a book of Jewish history and realized that she was merely keeping alive, on the streets of Queens, the centuries-old ghetto injunction to keep anything valuable hidden. From the goyim. She couldn't shake the notion she'd inherited that life was a battleground, that a pogrom could be cooked up around anyone's kitchen table and turn our quiet, safe, tree-lined streets into a killing field.

"Why do we have to go?" my sons whined in concert during the drive. I knew David felt like whining, too.

One of the most appealing philosophical stances of our synagogue was its commitment to holding open services for the New Year: anyone who felt the need to worship could walk in, pick up a prayer book, and take a seat. No one asked for a ticket or for proof of membership. As a result, our small congregation swelled enormously. Unable to accommodate everyone in our tiny sanctuary, we rented space in the gym of a local Roman Catholic church.

The parking lot was full by the time we drove up, the local streets clogged with cars. It reminded me of the scene at my father's synagogue on the High Holy Days.

"Let's just go home," Ben suggested. I was on the verge of giving in and giving up when I saw a spot and parked. As we walked toward the church entrance, shepherding our boys, making sure they didn't kick rocks with their feet, or jostle each other, or otherwise call attention to themselves, I remembered how my father looked on those occasions when we were all together at services—as if he finally had us exactly where he wanted us.

"All these people are Jewish?" Jake asked. He was incredulous. What a different world he's growing up in, I realized. When I was in elementary school, all my friends and I stayed home on the series of holidays following Rosh Hashanah, and as a result only two or three kids showed up in school. Jake was one of only two Jewish children in his class.

Had I lived my entire life, until now, in a ghetto? Or maybe I'd simply surrounded myself with a personal ghetto, friends who were mostly Jewish, or those who had such a sympathy for Jews that I never had a single moment of feeling persecuted or feeling like "the other." Not until I moved to Suffolk County with my family did I realize that others were defining me as a Jew even if I wasn't. That I had no control over how I was perceived. That to some people the fact that I was Jewish was the most salient feature about me.

In the vestibule hung a huge, homemade sign: "Welcome to Our Jewish Brothers and Sisters." The cacophonous swirl of conversation was utterly familiar. I picked up prayer books and led my family into the gym. On the stage stood the rabbi, swathed in a voluminous white robe and a tallis, which looked more like a colorful blanket woven in Santa Fe than the traditional white prayer shawl trimmed with blue that men wore during services. All the crucifixes were thoughtfully covered with dropcloths. The gym was packed. No pews or special seats, everyone sat on metal folding chairs, a democracy of sorts. An usher escorted us to seats way in the back. Please, I prayed silently, let these services be different from what I was used to. Let them mean something to me. Let them move me to prayer.

As we settled into our seats, my heart sank. We could barely see the rabbi, hardly hear. The sound system worked spottily; the air-conditioning sputtered. The prayer book in my lap was unfamiliar; I remembered none of the responsive readings from my father's synagogue. Most disappointing of all, I didn't know any of the melodies. Singing along, even though I hadn't known the words, had always been the most moving part of services for me. I wondered if we'd missed the shofar but was too embarrassed to ask our neighbors.

This wasn't working. No sooner did I arrive at services than I wished I were somewhere else—it always happened. The congregation was responsively reading a prayer in English, and I felt curiously, almost perversely, unmoved. I read along but in a low voice, mumbling, just to break the monotony. What kind of spiritual sustenance did exercises like this provide? Something was wrong with me, I knew; I couldn't penetrate to the core of the prayer. Maybe there were too many people around, too many distractions. And reading words written by someone else, intoning them together, seemed the antithesis of soulfulness. I closed the book louder than I intended to, frustration seeping out of me.

"How much longer do we have to stay?" Ben hissed. My sons' heads seemed to repel yarmulkes. Prayer books kept sliding off their laps. What was I thinking when I brought them here? David looked straight ahead, not at me.

The services were far from seamless; like a variety show, people shuffled off and on the stage, arks had to be opened and closed, blessings said and repeated. People around me rose, sat down, walked in and out, talked and waved at friends, smiled at children. Now the stage was being set for the blowing of the shofar. We hadn't missed it after all.

First came a few phrases in Hebrew, a kind of chanted command, then the clipped, punctuated toots of the animal horn. "Forgive us for the sins we have committed before Thee," the prayer begins. Repentance for Jews isn't so much a breast-beating affair; in fact, the Hebrew word for repentance is more accurately translated as "a turning." I always liked that idea, as if atonement were just around the corner, a quarter turn away, as if the tiniest tilt in perspective would enable you to behave differently in the coming year. As we stood together and recited the ancient words, I couldn't help but think of all the times I'd heard them intoned. And I couldn't help but take comfort from the fact that Ellen in Washington, D.C., and Nancy in New York City and my mother in Syosset and my sister in Tampa, all the people closest to me, were sitting in their own shuls and hearing the same sounds and words.

"I have to go to the bathroom," Jake said when we sat back down. I guided him out of the gym into the hall, where hundreds of people milled about. I smiled at those I knew and marveled at all I didn't, wondering what private reason had propelled everyone to get up as early as we had, get dressed, and assemble here. My parents never understood those people who came to shul only to stand in the lobby, on the outskirts of services, and disapproved of the festive, slightly carnival atmosphere that hovered around the fringes of synagogues on the High Holy Days. I relished it. I loved the sense that the hours-long service was like the ocean, something you dip into and come out of, only to return to when you feel like it. I enjoyed services most from this distance. Oddly, though I personally couldn't pray in a multitude, I enjoyed seeing others so absorbed. I liked being in the neighborhood of prayer.

Maybe my inability to feel spiritually transported during the actual service wasn't as much of a personal failing as I'd always assumed. I didn't feel especially close to God—my most intense spiritual moments still occurred when I was alone, reading, walking on the beach, reading a poem late at night in my study—but I did feel close to my brother and sister Jews, to this unwieldy, loud, colorful group of strangers who through some strange quirk of identity and history weren't total strangers. This feeling had a kind of spirituality all its own, one I couldn't achieve by myself; I had to be here to sample its variety.

Jake and I returned to services just in time to hear the stirrings of a thread of melody I remembered from my father's shul. Gradually, as if we'd all forgotten the words, only to rediscover them in tandem—"Oh yes, that's how it goes, I remember now"—memory rising from our feet, the congregation's voices swelled in the smelly, airless gym to a gusty, full-throated crescendo that filled every available cubic millimeter of space. I closed my eyes, swayed to the music, felt its power in my bones. Slowly our voices died back to a whisper, though the echo lingered. I couldn't remember the last time I'd had such a transporting moment surrounded by so many people.

Next we sat down, picked up our prayer books, began reading again. At least we were moving along at a brisk pace. When I was a girl, services—any service—seemed interminable. I remembered sitting in synagogue and feeling as if time had literally stopped. Now the pages flew by. Had the service been abridged? Or was I simply older?

I'd resolved to leave during the next break in the action, but then I saw, walking down the center aisle of the gym, the former president of the synagogue, the woman who'd presided over the first board meeting I'd attended when we'd decided to affiliate with Habitat for Humanity. Tall, regal, she made her slow way to the front of the room and, taking her graceful time, mounted the few steps to the stage to address about a thousand people. "Dear Friends," she began. Never had I seen someone look more at home. She thanked the church for its hospitality, spoke of her own wishes for the New Year, and articulated her feelings of gratitude for belonging to such a vital community. She spoke personally, from the heart—no officious tone, no false heartiness, no warmed-over jokes. In closing, she assured us that she and her husband wished us all a good year, full of health and challenges. Then she made her slow, proud way back to her family.

We were a sea of families. Parents shushed little children; showed off their college-age kids home for the holidays, some with girl- and boyfriends in tow; tended to elderly grandparents. My family may have been squirmy, inattentive, and restless, but at least we were together.

The buzz from the multitudes grew louder: the rabbi's sermon was approaching. My kids would never make it through. "Okay," I said to my sons and husband. "We can go."

"Finally," Ben said, annoyed beyond words.

"Thank God," Jake said.

After the services of my childhood, my family would eat a big lunch, then spend the rest of the day reading or taking a walk in our good clothes, every Jewish holiday a secular Sunday. When my husband and sons and I arrived home, we immediately changed into our casual clothes; the rest of the day, I knew, would be like any other.

"Thanks for agreeing to come," I said to David as he

headed downstairs for lunch. I knew he'd gone because I asked him to, just as I had dutifully, if somewhat resentfully, accompanied my parents years ago. "I'm not even sure why I bothered to go."

"You don't have to explain it," he said.

I wanted to explain it—not to him, but to me. That I felt good about having gone, and not merely as if I'd discharged a duty, was what puzzled me most of all. It wasn't as if the services had inspired me any more than they had in the past. What was different, I thought, was that I hadn't let my lack of prayerfulness distract me, derail me.

So what if the prayers still seemed mechanical, so what if we didn't stay the entire time, so what if I found less spiritualism in the services themselves than in their accoutrements. This year I'd widened my sights, drawn comfort where I could find it: the sight of all of us coming together, milling about in the lobby, singing together, studying each other's families, smiling at each other as if to say, "I don't know you, but you're not a stranger. You look familiar. We could sit down, this minute, right here, and talk."

This was a spiritual moment as valid as any other, I thought, taking off my grandmother's diamond engagement ring and putting it away until next year, just as my mother did—the realization that we seemed so small a presence at every other time, scattered as we were in our little communities, on our residential streets. Yet there we were, an antidote to the Diaspora, a metaphoric nation within a nation. I was moved to tears just to think about it—even though I knew my reaction smacked of the very tribalism that had in the past infuriated me.

"But *why?*" Though we were nearly sixteen, high school juniors, my friends and I sounded whiny as two-year-olds, our question echoing off the walls of the cramped, cinder-block basement classroom with increasing urgency. We slapped our hands on the desks in pure exasperation, rolled our eyes, mugged putting our heads down on our desks as if to say "We give up."

At the desk in the front of the room, absorbing our blows, sat Rabbi Witty, pale and slightly sweaty. Pound for pound, hormone for hormone, we should have overpowered him. There were about ten of us, fueled by a collective skepticism, bent on sharpening our philosophical teeth on the whetstone of his unshakable beliefs. Yet he managed to hold us off, or at least to keep us in check. Though far from svelte, he was tall, younger in retrospect than we realized at the time, and didn't look like an Orthodox Jew; in fact, you wouldn't at first even notice the little yarmulke miraculously adhering to the back of his head no matter how he moved, or the fringes of the garment religious men wear under their shirts sticking out between his dark, sagging pants and white, tieless shirt.

More mental boxing match than seminar, this class at my father's synagogue was my first formal course in Judaism. I'd enrolled, and convinced several friends to enroll, after my father suggested that I consider it. Much to his surprise, I agreed, out of an intuitive sense that it's always wise to know one's enemy.

"Jewish Philosophy" was its formal title, but I remember very little actual philosophy. Though I'm sure Rabbi Witty's curriculum was wide-ranging—he was very intelligent and brimming with enthusiasm—all I recall, in true teenage fashion, were our discussions about sex. Why were women considered unclean when they menstruated? we demanded of him. Why couldn't women touch men when they were menstruating? Why couldn't married couples sleep together whenever they wanted? Why did a two-week period of abstinence increase desire?

Patiently, as if grateful for the challenge with which we provided him, as if we were doing him a favor, he tried to explain the laws of family purity, as he called them, ancient rules governing when husband and wife could have relations, the value of self-restraint. I could see him struggle—he paused, looked into the distance, studied his hands, began, stopped, changed tactics. He wanted us to understand. I could see that he was a good, decent man, that he was living his life according to a set of rules that somehow enhanced and elevated it.

At our desks, emboldened by our numbers, we sat back and affected world-weariness, as if we'd had sex thousands of times, as if our virginity were only a technicality, a minor glitch, as if the amount of time we'd devoted to imagining the erotic arts had made us connoisseurs and left him the virgin, the sexual naïf. This was 1968, after all. We were interested not in reining in our impulses but in giving them free rein, not self-control but loss of control, not apportionment but satiety.

His inexhaustible willingness to begin anew, to explain again, time after time, only distilled our disdain. Yet we continued to show up every Thursday evening, when we could have been on the phone gossiping about boys, planning our next action against the war, working for Eugene McCarthy—and so did he. This was the first time I'd actually met, talked with, and come to know a rabbi away from his pulpit. By day he was the principal of a secular elementary school; he was just like the teachers I encountered in the classroom, had crushes on, spent hours thinking about. How tired he must have been, I now realize, how badly he must have needed the money to schlep from Queens to teach a room full of ungrateful suburban girls who thought they knew everything. We treated him with far less courtesy than we extended to our teachers in school, knowing that he wouldn't grade us, that he would always welcome us, would never fail us no matter how badly we mocked him, how snottily we turned our philosophical backs to him, how derisively we spat on his ideal of Jewish family life. But was he never a teenager? Didn't he remember what it was like?

"February 1968. Dear Wally," I wrote, as I did every couple of weeks, to a former junior high school English teacher who stood in the opposite corner of the ring from Rabbi Witty in my personal boxing match, the man who single-handedly introduced me to the sixties, to the need to question everything received, to take nothing at face value, to examine and be critical. He'd left his job teaching in a suburban school district to settle in North Carolina, and I regularly wrote him letters brimming with heated intensity in which I confided my most apostate thoughts. He never failed to take me seriously; he never intimated, as did every other grown-up with whom I had anything approaching a serious discussion, that I'd change my mind when I was older, that I'd see the light, repudiate everything I was about to espouse. It was less that he failed to notice the ten-year difference in our ages than that he knew age didn't necessarily confer wisdom. He was the only adult I knew who wasn't tethered to a family, to job security; in short, he didn't think of the future as a train he needed to board lest he find himself left behind at a deserted station with only his suitcase to sit on.

A few weeks ago we experienced a major spiritual revelation around here. . . . I heard about this mystical sect in Judaism, called Kaballah. Just from some reading in the encyclopedia, I found all kinds of great facts. First of all, the Kaballah was a sect that has pretty much died since the 12th century in Spain where it flourished. The Zohar, a book that explains the philosophy, has never been fully translated from the Aramaic. But most Jewish scholars today profess little or no knowledge. The dogmas deal with getting closer to the Godspirit. They have a vast system of numerology worked out, like astrology, but this seems to be secondary to their main belief. Kaballah was a kind of resistance to the rationalism and legalism of Maimonides. Then I found references to the Theosophical Society and the gnostics, which in turn gave me references to the Upanishads. Another point, the Essenes, the sect of Jesus, was basically the same as the Kaballah, and this is what Christ had to have drawn upon for his philosophy. I was really excited; in *Franny and Zooey* Seymour remarked that all legitimate religious study must lead to the same thing: the unlearning of all illusionary differences. It seems to be that if you take any religion back to its origins, you will end up in the same place. So I guess Eastern mysticism is composed only of what the Western religions try to play down, but essentially, it is made up of the same stuff.

Needless to say, Rabbi Witty was not interested in hearing about how all religions are made up of the same "stuff," or emanated from the same source, as Joseph Campbell's books on world mythology so convincingly argued. Neither was he interested in mysticism and the Zohar and the parts of Judaism expunged from orthodoxy. He grew impatient when we raised these points; he half closed his eyes as he would in reaction to too loud rock music, as if they caused him physical distress.

Nor did he want to hear particularly how the Old and New Testaments were related—news that I took special pleasure in relating. I'd learned about it in my high school "Bible as Literature" class: "A portion in Isaiah is practically telling the complete life of Christ, from his ancestry to crucifixion, but the Jewish scholars interpret it differently; they claim that the man depicted is all the Jewish people," I wrote to Wally. "It seems somehow so wrong for this natural continuity to be broken up by organized religion. The connections between the two testaments were so strong and sinewy, impossible to deny, a single book, one presaging the other, one the fulfillment of the earlier."

But comparative religion was a luxury, an acquired taste Rabbi Witty didn't have the time to cultivate; his plate was already overloaded by the burdens of a career, a family, and daily fulfillment of the 613 commandments required of each Orthodox Jewish man. "Don't you wonder what it's like, going to a Catholic mass?" I asked him one evening. He shuddered visibly. Why look further, he told us, when everything you need, a universe of riches, is right in your own garden? Don't think about grand patterns, he told us. Judaism is about consecrating the everyday, about the holiness of ordinary life—eating, having relations . . .

Why *not* look beyond? we asked him back, exasperated beyond reason, answering question with question. We weren't interested in consecrating everyday life; we were living for the future and delving through the past for clues as to the commonality of all religion. Those who pigeonholed themselves into sectarian niches, like my parents, my friends' parents, and Rabbi Witty, seemed like those who denied that the earth was round, who turned their backs on the age of discovery, who refused, out of stubbornness and fear—fear that they'd betray those already dead—to look down the road and admit that they saw something majestic in the distance. They were hobbled by rationality, by a fundamental need to be linear, to have structure, partition, clear boundaries: the goyim and the Jews. But surely unlearning the differences had to be the goal of religion. And enshrining one religion over another seemed the worst folly, a sin against God.

Why are we Jewish? my friends and I asked ourselves. Wasn't it a simple accident of nature, a quirk, a roll of the dice that determined our birth into one family and not another? But surely that didn't mean I was fated to be Jewish, or Catholics Catholic. Finding the religion within which one found answers, which adequately explained the world, was much too important a task to be left to capricious assignment.

My parents wrung their hands, blamed themselves. If only they'd sent me to religious school. But I assigned no blame; in fact, I was grateful to have escaped indoctrination. I was happy to embark on a quest, to be a free thinker, to tackle the big issues with my friends. Together we concocted a homespun seminar on comparative religion. First we studied Christianity—reading the Gospels, attending mass. I was particularly attracted by irreducible mysteries—of the trinity, of the virgin birth—coiled at the inner heart of Catholicism, its magnanimity, its mercy, its beautiful music, not to mention the fact that they let girls dress up as beautiful brides.

But within months we became disenchanted with turning the other cheek and turned to Sartre: we read *What Existentialism Is* and agreed that our existence preceded our essence, that it was up to us to make our lives have meaning. When this proved bloodless, we journeyed to the Far East—an inescapable alternative in 1967—to read about Zen Buddhism, Lao-tse, and the Upanishads. Yes, we cried fervently, the path to happiness is to surrender our desires—at a time when we were burning up with desire for everything.

Of course, I wasn't simply running toward, but running away, and never was my flight more urgent than the afternoon my family traveled into New York City to see *Fiddler on the Roof.* No sooner did the curtain go up than my parents and everyone around me began sniffling, awash in reflexive nostalgia. To me, the play was no more moving than the evening news broadcast or a Friday night service. Living in the muddy, ramshackle ghetto, walking on unpaved streets, eating potatoes when you were lucky, working at the meagerest, most mundane jobs just to stay alive—this was the reality of life in the old country, romanticized beyond recognition, strutted across the stage as if we should desire it. As everyone around me melted into tears, I grew stony and ever more furious. "Go!" I shouted silently to the daughter who fell in love with a boy from the next town. "Go, get out, follow your heart. You have a right to live your own life."

Red eyed, weeping openly, the audience thundered to its feet for a standing ovation. "How true," they said to each other without speaking. Where are their brains? I thought to myself. How could anyone long for the old country? Did they forget that Jews hadn't chosen to live together, in the nice, cozy ghetto, but had been forced into it? Did they forget the stories their own parents had told them about life in the old country, the squalor, the backbreaking labor, the frigid winters, the hunger, the threat of pogroms, the treks an ancestor had undertaken to escape the terrifying grip of the law? What we saw on stage was a fairy tale, a sterile, sanitized commercial.

We tumbled out into the lobby, into the street, an overdressed, slightly hysterical, conspicuous throng, insistent on showcasing, on flaunting, those traits that most clearly branded us, that nauseated me. Yiddish flowed, thick and viscous. Even my father had begun slipping into Yiddishisms lately. It was bad enough when my mother and grandmothers went on about *punim*s (faces) and *pupik*s (belly buttons)—it was a feminine language, after all, in its insistence on bodily things, on secrets. In my father's mouth it sounded unnatural, revolting, positively perverse, bespeaking a desire to be old before his time, to walk stooped over, to be proud of the fact that you lived in a closet or that you dribbled gravy on your clothes when you aged.

"Anyone who saw me with my family," wrote the literary critic Anatole Broyard in a 1979 essay, "knew too much about me." I too longed to break away, to begin a new, clean page—to *pass*—as if I ever could. As if my Jewish name, hair, nose, accent, outlook, cast of thought and attitude, could ever be mistaken for anything else.

God, how I hated being a Jew. Hated being branded, being different, having to follow laws and rules I could never live up to. My roiling self-hatred, the fact that I'd become a virulent anti-Semite, was a secret I kept locked within me, for I didn't understand it. Yet I couldn't figure out why my parents didn't hate themselves as well, why they were most concerned with perpetuating my misery.

For it all came down to intermarriage, the scourge of the Jewish people. I couldn't count how many sermons I'd sat through—at the synagogue, and at my parents' kitchen table—about the perils of assimilation, of losing our beloved, jealously guarded identity, all because too many Jewish boys and girls were thoughtless enough to fall in love with someone who wasn't of our faith.

By the time I was twelve I knew the score. "It would kill them"—my parents, I meant—I wrote in my seventh-grade diary, after Johnny Kalagaros, my first boyfriend, kissed me. Three years later, when Michael Moraia began calling for me on Saturday nights, and I watched my parents barely act civilly to him, I was much angrier. How dare they care more about the perpetuity of Judaism than my own personal happiness?

We argued endlessly, passionately. "What if?" I would taunt them. What if I met a man whom I loved with all my heart, in some mythical future, and he wasn't Jewish? Would they want me to give him up? Would they boycott my wedding? Would they sit shiva for me? Well, too bad; I was bloody well going to marry whomever I wanted. True love knew no religious boundaries. To their *Fiddler on the Roof* medley I juxtaposed *West Side Story*'s "One Hand, One Heart"—"When love comes, a storm. There is no right or wrong. Your love is your love!"

"Blood is thicker than water." That was my parents' perennial parting shot, their closing salvo in this argument, which took place in installments, spanning my entire adolescence. They averted their eyes; privately they must have wondered what they had done to deserve an obstreperous daughter like me.

But Rabbi Witty didn't mind taking me on, and that, finally, is why my friends and I continued to show up in his class, week after week, showering him with objections, pelting him with our derision. He was our father yet not our father, and that freed him to roar, "Yes! You'd have to give him up. Find a Jewish boy."

"Never!" we'd retort, digging in, fighting the hegemony, trying to keep it from wiggling its tentacles into the most private recesses of our lives.

Yet he never turned away from us. He never stopped trying to reach us. He never tired of thinking of ways to explain how wrongheaded we were. He never lost patience with us; he viewed the failure as his. The more objections we raised, the harder he tried, every outburst provoking the opposite of what we intended, like a knot that kept getting tighter the more I pulled at it. His admonitions to stay indoors felt confining, as if he had maneuvered me into a half nelson. "Let me go, let me go," I said to him silently, countless times, with the same exasperation and indignation I brought to conversations with my father. "How dare you tie me down, how dare you touch me. Don't come near me!"

The louder I spoke, the more I struggled, the more, it seemed, he loved me. One night, in the midst of another argument about love and sex, I felt particularly reckless. "What will happen when your daughter"—I knew he had a baby girl—"comes home with a *goyishe* boy?"—using the term I despised. "And she says that this is the boy she wants to marry?"

"It won't happen," he said. He spoke calmly, but I saw that a vein in his neck was pulsing. I saw him reach for the fringe on the undergarment as a child would reach for a teddy bear. "It simply won't happen," he said, speaking very softly now. "That scenario just wouldn't be part of her world."

"You're deluding yourself," I said. I spoke to him as I would to no other grown-up. That was the last thing I said all night.

But as we walked out of class, he approached me and put his arm around me. He spoke softly, affectionately. "You know, of everyone here, you'll be the *rebbetzen* one day"—a rabbi's wife. To him, this was the highest honor, the paramount achievement. But I saw a woman in a shapeless dress and wig bent over the stove, honored because of how well she married, not because of herself. This was the last straw, the unforgivable prophecy—the voice I rebelled against for the next ten years, through college and graduate school, until I met David, and we decided to get married.

"So," began Rabbi Schwartz. I was at yet another evening meeting at the synagogue, this one for the parents and teachers of those children who would turn thirteen sometime during the coming year. "Who among you is making your first Bar or Bat Mitzvah?" We novices were clearly in the majority, all of us looking vaguely terrified, as if we were embarking on a trek up Mount Everest.

It was the day after Halloween; a big plate of candy sat in the middle of the table. I studied the faces of the other parents, trying to match them with their kids, and realized how few families I knew despite the fact that our children had been in class together for five years. I remembered all the calls I'd received asking me to attend Shabbat class dinners, to be a class mother. Those who had taken advantage of these opportunities to meet sat together whereas I sat alone, off to the side.

Yet I was familiar with the new building—which now boasted peaceful mauve walls, a breathtaking cedar ceiling—while many other families, who hadn't been here since last spring, gasped as they entered. All of us had joined the synagogue when it looked shabby; we not only embraced it for its plainness, but congratulated ourselves for not caring about facades, for burrowing beneath the evident tackiness and discovering the unchanging essence. But now that it was beautiful—and it was, in a subtle, understated way—we were afraid to love it, as if we were loving it for the wrong reasons.

Our feelings about our children were undergoing a similar shift. Caught up in a tumult of early adolescence, they were changing all too rapidly, and our feelings about them were sometimes frightening. You could almost hear the whir of mental calculators: when our children began Hebrew school, they were seven and eight years old, and we were closer to thirty than forty. Now they talked on the phone and put cream on their pimples; they told private jokes and strode through the house with the vigor of ten men. "You have wrinkles, Mom," my son teased me with an edge of hostility. He was almost as tall as I was, negating the height advantage I'd enjoyed since he was born, slowly but relentlessly erasing the disparity between us. You don't realize until you come face-to-face with the irrefutable evidence that you're on a seesaw: as our children ascend into young adulthood, we descend slowly into middle age.

Up until now, I'd been able to entertain the comforting illusion that Ben and I were one flesh. I could read his mind, see thoughts flicker across his eyes. But lately he'd become more secretive; he kept his own counsel. He accumulated a network of friends, just as I had at his age, with whom he spoke every night, behind closed doors. Suddenly, painfully, I was persona non grata.

Even more dramatically, he was developing physically, turning into a man right before my eyes, leaving the orbit of the relationship we'd created. He was becoming his own person. A not me. He'd become self-conscious. He had his own beliefs, experiences, his own way of doing things, of which I knew very little. Coming up against the hard kernel of his existence, that part I was excluded from, I wanted both to clutch him more tightly and push him away—exactly my feelings about making this Bar Mitzvah.

"Does everyone have a copy of 'The Kehillath Shalom Semi-Complete Bar and Bat Mitzvah Guide'?" asked Rabbi Schwartz, directing us to the first page. He explained that in olden times, children who turned thirteen were considered adults, responsible for themselves, capable of clear judgment. Adolescence is such a modern concept, I thought. Our ancestors passed from childhood into adulthood, without any way station or rehearsal.

"Furthermore," he continued, "a child becomes a Bar or Bat Mitzvah, literally, a 'child of the commandment,' simply by turning thirteen." A ceremony, a party, is all for the parents, a recognition that children, especially firstborns, become their parents' sundials. "You understand what I'm telling you? You don't have to do anything else. You can cancel all your party plans. You become a Bar Mitzvah automatically."

He was being facetious, but I wasn't. Maybe it was time for me to can it all, to bail out. As June 3, 1995, loomed closer, as the need to call a caterer, a photographer, to sign contracts and leave deposits grew more pressing, I was besieged by a spell of second-guessing and inertia. Just a month earlier, when my family gathered at our house to break the fast after Yom Kippur, I'd blown up after my mother innocently asked, "So, how are preparations coming along?"

"Yes, we have to know how many people we can invite, we have out-of-town people to think about," my mother-in-law chimed in.

That was all it took. I launched into a tirade about how preparations weren't coming along; that I didn't want even to begin the process; that I had no time and no inclination at all to plan a party of this scale and the hell with it.

The house was entirely silent. None of us, including me, had realized how deep my antipathy ran.

My mother changed the subject.

"I wasn't kidding," I said to David later that night as we got ready for bed. "I can't stand thinking about it. Any of it. I don't have the time or energy for it. I don't even want to go shopping for a dress. I hate all those dresses you wear to these things"—the two-piece outfits in slinky material, the pert jacket covering the sequin-studded bodice, shoes and pocketbook dyed to match—which had suddenly come to symbolize everything that was wrong with Bar Mitzvahs as I knew them.

"You don't have to have that kind of dress," David reminded me. "Wear something else. Wear your wedding dress."

My wedding dress. I searched through my closet and there it was, hanging under dry-cleaner plastic—not a formal bridal gown, but a simple white dress with a floral pattern, a slip and overdress with a row of fabric-covered

buttons down the front, and a scoop neck—the most feminine, romantic dress I'd ever owned. David and I had bought
it together at Lord & Taylor, and I remembered everything
about it: seeing it on the rack, holding my breath until we
found the right size, the saleswoman who draped it over her
arm and ushered me into the fitting room, zipping me into
the form-fitting slip, buttoning each button, tying the belt,
the way David sat on the couch and how he nodded when he
saw me. Yes, we both agreed in an instant, this was perfect.
Exactly what we'd had in mind.

I pulled it off its hanger, held it up to me, and in an impulsive moment stepped out of my nightgown. I sucked in
my stomach, held my breath, and pulled at the zipper. There.
It still fit, if a little tight in the bosom. That's what breast-
feeding two children will do.

"I suppose I could wear this," I said to David.

"It looks good," he said. "And if you do, we won't have
to hire a photographer, we can just recycle our wedding
photos."

Well, why not, I thought, going to sleep. A ritual's a ritual; essentially, one rite of passage is the same as the next.
And this dress had a good track record.

"Turn to page ten," Rabbi Schwartz was saying. " 'Re-
quirements for Bar/Bat Mitzvah.' " Apparently, we'd finished
with the spiritual part of the evening's discussion and landed

squarely in the realm of more earthly considerations—fees, timetable of events, questions of who will offer prayers during the service, who will usher, who will present the tallis, who will speak in which order, where to position the flowers, whether or not to hire a cantor.

Innumerable decisions, a mountain of minutiae; my frantically scribbled notes filled page after page. The more I wrote, the angrier I became. To worry about seating plans was to lose sight of the day's meaning. I sighed loudly to register my protest against getting my hands dirty with all these details; across the table, a woman looked up and locked me into her gaze. Together we widened our eyes in disbelief and imperceptibly nodded our heads as if to say "No way I'll get through this."

When the meeting was over, we took our time leaving, congratulating and commiserating with one another in the corridor, on the porch, in the parking lot. We questioned one another like fledgling district attorneys: "Where are you having yours? How many people?" One woman nodded sympathetically as I relayed my problems with the unwieldy guest list. "Try making a Bat Mitzvah and getting a divorce at the same time," she said, trudging to her car.

A *haimish* crowd, I said to myself, buckling my seat belt—a friendly, warm, welcoming group of people. People I didn't have to worry about, people I could be myself with. Funny, to have this Yiddish word bubble up. Funnier still that I didn't seem to mind. The word seemed absolutely right; no other would do. Why not use it? Why not say it aloud? I'd been noticing more and more Yiddish creeping into my interior conversations.

It was a cloudless night. To get home I had to first drive through the town of Huntington, sleepy and almost deserted by ten at night. How many times had I driven this route—in pouring rain, sleet, with a headache, distracted by an important phone call I had to cut short or thoughts of what to throw together for dinner—just to get Ben to and from Hebrew school?

How could I possibly quantify all the effort and energy that I'd devoted to my son since his birth? It wasn't simply a matter of adding up hours—though every parent I knew did so, calculating how many hours we spent at work, how many with the kids, hoping for just the right balance. But what about the time you spend thinking about your child? What about the moments when you're teaching a class or writing a letter and suddenly you wonder where he is, if he's all right, if he's being teased or put down, if his ear is bothering him, if he's eating his lunch or throwing it away, if the girl he likes looks at him or laughs at him. The time you spend at the candy store trying to divine which candy bar will bring him the most pleasure, or doing an extra wash so he'll have his special sweatshirt to wear the next day. How could you possibly add all that up? I conceptualized that total in terms not of a number, but of weight, of volume, of mass. It was a crushing entity, an enormous presence in my life. I'd marshaled so much of my own energy and resources to keep him alive, to see him thrive, to be sure he'd embrace the gift of life we'd thrust upon him. He'd been the organizing principle of my life since the moment he appeared, Mohican head first.

I wanted the sum of all my effort and caring externalized; I wanted it to be somehow made concrete, to appear before me, so I could admire it, so I could stand in awe of it, stroke it, poke it, feel its density, its heft, its impossible weave, and say, "Yes, I made that, I kept that going, and every second it grows larger and larger." I wanted to palpate it, to probe it with my hands like an internist looking for liver and kidneys; like a cardiologist, I wanted to position my stethoscope in the exact spot to hear the thunderous heartbeats.

When Ben was younger, I didn't have this need. Why now? Maybe because I felt him moving away—because a seismic shift was occurring not simply in Ben, but within our family, the four-cornered unit we'd nurtured all these years. The firm foundation we'd built was being rocked by underground forces; its boundaries were breaking down. I could foresee, in Ben's incipient teenage rebellion, that he would one day leave our family behind—as he should, as his bother would. But that would leave David and me alone. Maybe I had turned to the synagogue sensing that I needed to enlarge my very definition of family; I was seeking to establish, through my slowly increasing involvement in its day-to-day life, a meta-family, encompassing three generations, which would abide, which would welcome me, absorb me. Maybe that's what my father had sought as well, a family that wouldn't cast him off, leave him behind.

By the time I swung onto Roller Coaster Road, the radio station was playing a set of tunes by Frank Sinatra—my mother's favorite. Though I made a great show of hating him when I was a teenager—how else could a self-respecting girl, born in 1952, who came of age during the British invasion, have acted?—I listened to my mother's albums in secret not for his voice, but because of the songs he sang, for the delight of the lyrics. "I've got you under my skin," he sang in his best barroom swagger. Second to singing in the shower, I loved singing along to the car radio. If Ben were with me, he'd look at me with the same derisive look I gave my mother years ago as she dusted, merrily and atonally singing along with Frankie. She was younger then, I realized with a start, than I was now.

"But before I do, just the thought of you makes me stop

before I begin," I sang, my voice suddenly cracking, and the tears I'd squelched all night spilled out. Suddenly I was older than my mother, my son was my peer; time fractured, revealed itself to be the fiction that it is. So did distance. I wasn't in fact going home or going anywhere but in a huge circle. One day soon Ben would bring home girls for us to meet. I couldn't pretend that the question of their religion wouldn't matter to me. I cared about having Jewish grandchildren, about preserving our identity; in fact, I never cared more. For without boundaries there is only the chaos of time, and we are at its mercy. Roller Coaster Road indeed.

Two months later I found myself hosting a diminutive version of our family's traditional Hanukkah party. Usually we gathered at my mother's, but this year she'd announced that she wasn't up for it, which was actually fine with me. I didn't mind visiting her at her house with the kids and David, but the few parties she'd hosted since my father had died were positively haunted, and now that my sister and her family had moved to Tampa the gathering would feel even more bereft. And my in-laws, en route to Florida to wait out the rest of the winter, were consumed with packing, not cooking.

"*Baruch ata Adonai,*" we said together—my mother and David's parents were with us—intoning the prayers over the candles, kissing each other Happy Hanukkah, before letting Ben and Jake at their presents. Then we sat down to eat, David and I at the head of the table. This was our party. Observing the holidays, keeping the faith—all this had landed in our lap. If we didn't do it, it wouldn't get done. Our parents had done their time; they'd passed the baton to us.

I felt myself well up with tears. Our family, it seemed, was being reconfigured as completely as the map of Central Europe. The concept of a family was all that remained constant; the people within it changed—died, were born, left for college, moved away, grew old and tired.

Who is in your family? How widely or narrowly do you cast your net? That was the essential, enduring question, the one we had to answer anew every few years. So many of the people we loved and depended on were no longer capable of responding when we called, time, distance, or death intervening. Yet our synagogue family would be there for us, to bring us food when we were ill, to visit us after a death. Sometimes you need a literal, physical neighbor. Sometimes you have to love the one you're with.

And I realized, at that moment, passing the applesauce for the latkes, why observing Ben's Bar Mitzvah was important to me: it would give us the opportunity to throw open the doors and invite everyone who cared about him—and not just him, but his parents, his grandparents as well—to show him how large his family was. These are the people with whom we'd cast our lot, whom he could rely on, to whom he could turn if he needed to. I wanted him to know, and to trust with perfect knowledge, that he'd never be entirely alone.

On a rainy January night, David and I drove to the synagogue about an hour before Ben was finished with Hebrew school to meet a caterer we'd called. Following the glow of his flashlight, we traipsed around the frozen yard while he marked off distances and made logistical calculations. "You could have eight, ten tables, tops," he said—I knew he was envisioning everything; in his eyes, a June garden party was unfolding, while I saw nothing but barren trees and dead grass—"Buffet tables here, the band and dance floor here, eight waiters . . . Yes," he announced definitively, adjusting his yarmulke—he was from a kosher caterer—"we can swing it."

I nearly hugged him. We repaired to the cramped vestibule of the shul, where he gave us his card and we jotted down information about menu possibilities, deposits, timetables, prices.

"Are you talking about having a tent in the yard for the Bar Mitzvah?" asked one of the women milling in the lobby with us, waiting for Hebrew school to be over. "What a lovely idea."

"It *is* a lovely idea," I said to David as we drove home, with our boys in the backseat.

"I'm having my Bar Mitzvah party in a tent?" Ben piped up. "A tent like the ones the ancient Israelites lived in?" Though he acted as if this were news, it wasn't—we'd kept him fully apprised of our plans. He'd agreed to all our proposals with an alacrity that left me slightly guilty: never having attended a Bar Mitzvah, he had no idea of what could have been involved.

His sudden if momentary interest, though, made me realize that I had very little sense of what he thought about not only the Bar Mitzvah, but being Jewish. Ever since he'd become friendly with a few kids in his Hebrew school class, his vociferous objections to going had cooled. He bridled at having to learn Hebrew but clearly relished theological discussions, particularly those led by the rabbi, who didn't seem to irritate him the way Rabbi Witty had irritated me. All in all, he didn't seem to find organized religion as objectionable as I had at his age. But I'd grown up surrounded by Jews, and he'd grown up on a block on which he felt conspicuously different. Among his friends at home he enjoyed his "outsider" status, but at Hebrew school he was one of the kids, Kehillath Shalom a place of refuge.

"A Bar Mitzvah in a tent," he said again, mulling it over. "Sounds weird. But possibly cool."

Within a week I'd called four caterers and received menus—just for comparison purposes—spoken to several photographers, and spent an hour in a local print shop, gazing through books of invitations. I kept careful notes in a special file folder and reported to David on my findings. Together we went through our guest list one last time. We had to pare it down drastically and hope that our friends who couldn't be invited would understand.

Before I fell asleep that night, I found myself composing another guest list, the antiguest list, containing the names of all the people who should be there but wouldn't be. David's sister Robbin and my father, of course, were first and second, but there were scores of other significant no-shows: friends we'd lost touch with, relatives and friends who had moved too far away, even those people with whom we'd had nasty fallings-out suddenly came to mind. David's old girlfriend and my old boyfriend, they too had a right to be there. It seemed, curiously, that just about everyone belonged on the list. "Each experience contains its opposite," my Shakespeare professor had taught me, and apparently each person we chose to invite evoked the ghost of another we couldn't.

"If only we could spend as much as we wanted," I said to David the next morning. "If only we could rent the lawn of a mansion, and invite everyone, and have the best food, and a ten-piece band with horns and a grand piano, and a photographer and a videographer. If only we didn't have to make all these decisions."

"But then the party would get away from us," David reminded me. "Making decisions is how we make it our own."

He was right. Personalizing this celebration was singularly important to me. I'd even planned on doing the calligraphy for the invitations myself, just as I'd done for our wedding. I retrieved my calligraphy pen, purchased graph paper, and for weeks practiced in spare moments at my desk. I toyed with different scripts, different wordings. But after a few weeks I realized my skills had atrophied. My attempts looked too amateurish, and I wanted the invitations to be beautiful.

Abandoning my calligraphy, I sought the expertise of a professional printer. Together we worked on wording and layout and finally settled on a version I liked:

*Please join us when our son*
*Benjamin Mark*
*is called to the Torah as a Bar Mitzvah*
*Saturday, June 3, 1995*
*Kehillath Shalom*
*Cold Spring Harbor, New York*
*Kiddush luncheon to follow services.*

Walking home from the copy store after leaving my deposit, I thought of the invitations being dispersed through the mail, landing in people's mailboxes, being opened, remarked upon, responded to. We'd taken our first official step, the one we couldn't retract. We were gathering the clan.

CHAPTER 5

# *Ritual*

undays we drive to the Bronx to see my grandparents. Usually we visit with them in their apartment off Kingsbridge Avenue, where I stand at their second-story window and pretend I can see Yankee Stadium. But certain Sundays we don't go upstairs. They come down, get in our car, and we drive to the cemetery.

My grandfather, as wide as he's tall, sits in front next to my father; my grandmother and mother, like bookends, each sit near a door in the backseat, my sister and I the slim volumes they contain. They both wear fur coats with blue satin linings, though my mother's fur is tightly curled and my grandmother's whispery soft. I always sit next to her. My grandmother is tall and imposing. Everyone says I am like her. We both had red hair when we were young. Now mine has turned brown and hers steel gray. She keeps her old braids wrapped in a coarse linen handkerchief at the bottom of her dresser drawer. I study them each time we visit. She lets me root around in her drawers. She has lots of treasures, little mirrors and combs and strands of beads, and no matter what question I ask her about them, like "Where did you buy these?" or "How old are these?" she smiles and says I can take them home, as if that were what I had asked.

In the car she lets me lean into her to touch her coat as we drive into Queens, the land of cemeteries. We always drive to the same gate, near some kind of building with smokestacks, and I wonder if there's a connection between it and dead bodies, but I never ask.

There are many things I would love to ask about but don't. Like why my sister and I have to wait in the car. Only the adults go into the cemetery. My grandfather returns before the others. He stands outside the car no matter how cold it is, and he never wears a hat, even though he's bald—only gloves and a muffler on really cold days.

My father is always walking between his mother and my mother when we spot them leaving the cemetery. They walk slowly, as if they don't want to leave. There are big sighs and groans all around as everyone settles back into the car, and no one talks. If my sister and I touch each other, we are told to stop, immediately, no one is in the mood. When we get back to my grandparents' apartment, everyone goes first to the bathroom to wash their hands. Next week we'll visit the other cemetery, where my grandfather's family is buried. And the week after that we'll take my mother's mother to visit her husband's grave and the graves of her sisters and brothers. And by the time we finish visiting everyone, it will be spring, time to start over.

"Please attend our Bar Mitzvah Class Family Day." Ben never remembered to give me the notices he received from his Hebrew school teachers; I had to stumble upon them, strewn as they were on his desk, dresser, or bedroom floor. "Bring a recipe, some photos, or a bit of memorabilia to class this Sunday, and be prepared to tell us a story about your family." Surprisingly, I didn't have a hard time convincing David that we should go.

"A full house," crowed Ben's Hebrew school teacher, for every family—siblings and all—showed up. We sat in a circle, each family clustered together like a diminutive tribe. Curiosity and familiarity quickly overcame our awkwardness. Four of us, for instance, had brought in a recipe for Russian coffee cake, and we all had the same tough time securing it.

Our grandmothers had relied on maddeningly inexact measurements—"some flour, and a little less sugar."

"I once spent an entire day shadowing my grandmother in her kitchen," one woman related, "and as she poured ingredients into the bowl I'd catch them in a paper towel, measure them, and write everything down. But even after all that, my mandelbrot still didn't come out right."

Many of us also brought sepia family photos. "Everyone's so dressed up in this," said one woman, holding up a picture and staring at it, as if perhaps this time it would speak to her in a way it hadn't before. "It was probably taken at a Bar Mitzvah or wedding."

"No one ever smiles in those old photos," one woman said, and I could hear, in my mind's ear, the mental page turning of twelve families as we scanned our families' photo albums and realized that this was true. In the old country, people approached the camera with solemnity.

"My grandfather was thirteen when he came to this country, by himself, and he never saw his family again," one man said. We all looked at our nearly thirteen-year-old children whom we didn't allow to travel to the mall on their own and tried to imagine them crossing an ocean, searching a dockside crowd for a cousin they'd never met who was supposed to meet them, walking down strange streets for the first time, hearing a language they couldn't speak. My grandparents had come to this country in 1903, roughly ninety years ago. Was that a long time or the blink of an eye?

After everyone spoke, we watched a videotape entitled *Gefilte Fish*—a cleverly intercut narrative about three generations of women and how they coped with the tradition of serving gefilte fish for Passover. A woman my grandmother's age complained how she had to go to three different fish stores to find the freshest pike and codfish and how she had worked to grind the fish and season it just right, but clearly she relished the task; her daughter, a woman my mother's age, also made her own fish but with much more anguish—wondering, for example, if grinding the fish in the food processor changed not only its texture and taste, but its symbolic meaning; and a woman my age displayed the jar of gefilte fish that she bought in the store and demonstrated how she put a piece of fish on a bed of lettuce with a dollop of horseradish, defying anyone to tell the difference.

"My grandmother made her own gefilte fish, and her own challah, and her own kreplach [dumplings], and her kitchen was the size of one of my closets," one woman said, wiping tears from her eyes.

"When I used to visit my grandmother in Brooklyn, we'd find cabbage soaking in the bathtub, batter in bowls in the closets, dough rising on the beds, wherever she could find an inch of space."

"My grandmother would knead her dough on a board she balanced on the windowsill in the kitchen," another woman said. "There was no other place to do it. She made the best bread. . . ." She trailed off, abandoning each of us to aromas we hadn't summoned up for years.

"And I have a kitchen which is three times the size of her entire apartment," she continued, rousing us out of our reveries, "and enough counter space to run a race on, and every appliance known to modern science, and I never cook! We get take-out nearly every night!" She sounded surprised, as if she'd just put these facts together, mildly outraged and, finally, sad. We all felt rueful, as if we were all on the verge of tearfully confessing, "But I'm doing the best I can!"

Secretly we feared that we had moved too far away from something precious; that by removing the labor of love from love, we had weakened love itself. This was a very modern sadness. Yet none of us wanted to lead our grandmothers' lives, or even our mothers'. In many ways they had the hardest task, the women's movement coming too late to help shape their ideas, but leaving them more than enough time to second-guess and, in some cases, repudiate how they'd structured their lives.

No, I wasn't about to glamorize housework, but neither was I going to deny the profound pleasure I derived from having a wonderful, well-prepared meal placed in front of me, of walking into a well-tended, well-kept house. The question wasn't whether to value it, but how to find ways to enable everyone to enjoy it, to partake of it, to create it for one another so that one person wasn't always in the kitchen or behind the vacuum. I remember how my grandmother collapsed into her seat at the seder table after depositing the last dish: she'd begun the grunt work that was her portion over a week earlier, when she scoured the kitchen, changed dishes, pots, and silverware from the ones she used every day to the special Passover sets, cleaned the house, moved the furniture she'd just polished so she could open the table. By the time she was done, the seder was just beginning. No wonder she could hardly stay awake. As we read about the Exodus from Egypt, she was dreaming of getting into her bed and going to sleep, her head nodding at a dangerous angle toward the chopped liver.

"My biggest regret," my grandmother solemnly told me when I came to visit her in the home where she spent her last years, "was that I never learned to drive."

Though she was perpetually in motion—cleaning, cooking, serving, walking, shopping—it was nonetheless staggering to envision her driving a car, and even more to realize her regret, her awareness of her position as someone who sacrificed on behalf of others. I'd always assumed sacrificial victims bore their burdens in silence, like the uncomplaining ram Abraham killed instead of Isaac.

"What was your first experience of knowing that you were Jewish?" Ben's teacher asked, as if she could read my mind. For visiting the cemetery was one of my first memories, as was the dual vision of grandmothers: one time traveling, lighting candles, speaking Yiddish, singing wordless songs; the other preparing food and dreaming of driving. These solitary, confined, regretful women, who gradually learned to confine themselves, bequeathed their religion to me.

David and I were quiet on the way home, both of us relishing the discussion, surprised by the intimacy that had arisen and taken root so quickly and effortlessly, upon which we would never have presumed, which overtook before we'd even noticed it. We'd bonded together as if we were fellow passengers on a ship crossing the sea to a new land, in which we were all celebrants in a ritual without precedent, one we were creating together.

All rituals, I realized, arise when the three normally parallel strands of time—past, future, and present—jump their tracks and collide head-on. Whether the ritual occurs daily, weekly, yearly, or over the span of a lifetime, it gives us the opportunity to remark on change—"Gee, last week when we had pancakes there was snow on the ground"; "The last time we met at a wedding you were pregnant"—within a context of constancy. Here we are again, still alive, still conscious.

My own family's rituals—going to the cemetery, Sabbath

dinners—remained stubbornly blind to time's passage; we became slave to ritual rather than its celebrants. Yet to pluck ritual from its historical context was to dull its resonance. For to focus on, to emphasize, either half of ritual's equation—the change or the constancy—renders it inert, impotent, and oppressive. Both have to be present for ritual to work its magic. For when it does, as it had that morning in Ben's class, it provides an escape hatch; you rise above any single feeling to find yourself simply feeling everything at once. You grow giddy waiting for your parents to emerge from the maw of the cemetery; you stop and watch a family of ducks cross the road on a sweltering July day en route to your father's funeral; you pause in the midst of foreplay and think, One day we will be old, one day we will die. This emotional state in which the emotions you experience have no name and coexist without negating each other is to the soul what air is to the body—that which we feed on, and rarely notice.

Two weeks later, during a January thaw, I met Alan, the man from the tent company the caterer had recommended, at the synagogue. He marked off the yard in paces, the way my father and husband measured out rooms in houses they considered buying, while I held a book of photos that showed the types of tents available. Did I want a solid color or a striped? If striped, blue and white, red and white, yellow and white? Did I want a tent with walls or without walls? With cathedral windows in the walls or regular windows? Oak dance floor? How large? What shape?

What kinds of tables did I want to rent? Round or rectangular? Seating ten or twelve? What kinds of tablecloths, napkins, silverware, serving pieces, hot plates, glasses? An open bar? Or champagne and wine?

What about the yarmulkes? Plain or decorated with braid? Ben's name written inside? His name and the date or just the name? Did we want it written in silver or gold? Did we want them delivered or picked up? Did we have a basket to put them in?

The decisions confronting me multiplied like the hydra; each one spawned three more. There were several ways to answer these questions. I could have said, "You decide. Whatever you think is best." Or I could have answered them quickly, off the top of my head. To think about each one, to take each seriously, was driving me crazy.

Gradually, though, over time, a criterion for making all these choices began to emerge. I'd choose the simplest, least expensive solution, unless our guests' comfort was involved. So we agreed to rent a canopy, from synagogue to tent entrance, just in case, God forbid, it rained. And we agreed on a sumptuous menu, because food was important to us. Would regular rather than cathedral windows on the tent walls impinge on our friends' comfort? Would tablecloths that didn't reach the floor? We didn't think so.

Furthermore, if we said yes to the tablecloths or to braided yarmulkes, we'd have to say no to something else—the extra desserts, for example. Suddenly being forced to operate within a limited budget seemed a welcome crucible: it forced me to take every decision seriously. It was tedious and agitating, but very clarifying. I was forced to stay focused, to articulate my values over and over and over again. If I could have said yes to everything, then nothing would have been as personal, nothing would have meant as much.

In January Ben turned thirteen. We bought him a new video game system he wanted, took him out to dinner, and sang "Happy Birthday" at home, over his favorite chocolate cake, which I always bake for him.

That night I hesitated at the threshold of his room. For the past thirteen years I'd always gone in to tuck him in, to sit with him a moment, to stroke his hair and talk about the day gone by, the one coming up. But one night, just a few weeks earlier, he'd stopped me cold at the door to his room. "You don't have to say good night to me anymore," he said, shifting in bed so his back was to me. "Maybe you haven't noticed, but I'm not a baby anymore."

Shaken, I told him in as calm a voice as I could muster that I'd been aware for some time that he was no longer a baby; this fact, however, had nothing to do with my wanting to say good night to him, a practice I fully planned on continuing even if only from where I stood, skewered by his icy words. He grunted his acquiescence. But after about a week of long-distance good-nights, he rustled his covers as I turned out the light and said, "Mommy doesn't want to come in?" sounding for all the world like a toddler.

Which child will greet me tonight? I wondered on the night of his birthday as I climbed the stairs to his room. I recalled what the rabbi had said, about how a child becomes Bar Mitzvah, literally, a son or daughter of the commandment, by attaining this age. He doesn't have to do anything else; simply be.

"Come in," Ben said, as I hoped—always hoped—he would. That evening, with each passing minute on his alarm clock drawing him closer to the cusp of adolescence, he was as playful as an eighteen-month-old—wanting me to tickle him, to tell him funny stories, to mangle words, to remember games we hadn't shared in years—so innocent, his cheek still smooth, his eyes dark and eager, still open to the world.

It seemed, for a moment, that Ben looked oldest the moment he was born, the first time I saw him, the scrawny shrunken face, the jet black hair plastered flat on his head with the womby oils and liniments, his eyes ancient as anything I've ever seen, as old as my birthdayless grandmother, who died, frail as a feather, sometime during her late seventies.

A few months from now, Ben would stand up in front of nearly everyone he knew and say, in his own words, "Today I am a man." Yet tonight he wanted nothing more than to hear baby stories: how he'd sneak out of bed and open the door to his room a crack to eavesdrop on *The Cosby Show;* how we lost and then recovered his beloved stuffed animal Minnie from a muddy Upper West Side intersection. "The past," Faulkner wrote, "isn't dead. It isn't even the past."

Birthdays, death days; first steps, first words, last words, first kisses: if you've ever fallen in love or had a baby or watched someone die, you know that these are made-up milestones, convenient fictions. As much as I love the story of Ben's first steps—how, one morning when he was nine months old and I was on the phone he wobbled into the kitchen—it is more myth than fact, a shorthand for what really happened; how, each morning for the past three months, he'd made microscopic progress toward his goal, successively approximating his upcoming breakthrough, creeping up to it, advancing one scintilla of a frame at a time.

Nature itself is gateless. Coiled within the first day of

winter lies the nascent kernel of summer; the seasons, with cold snaps in August and January thaws, make mockery of our need to delineate. And time is never a highway, but rather a ceaseless, recursive current with terrifying swirling eddies and peaceful tributaries, and you're never sure exactly where your fragile canoe will run aground. So you plan parties and rituals, just for the relief of having the earth beneath your feet, if only for a little while.

"Where can we plug in our electrical cords?" asked Simon, the caterer. "What type of chair do you want to rent?" Chairs? What kinds of choices could there possibly be?

"Where can we store the tables and chairs?" asked Alan, the tent man.

"When can the flowers be delivered?" asked the florist.

"What color napkins do you want in the bathroom?" asked Fran, the synagogue's caretaker.

"What's your theme?" asked the DJ we reluctantly hired—a live band was too expensive, and the alternative, a party without music, seemed too amorphous.

"Our theme is Judaism," David said. What else?

Ben began receiving invitations to Bar and Bat Mitzvahs from his Hebrew school classmates, and I realized with a shock that these were the first occasions he'd attended. When I was his age, oversized, hand-lettered invitations arrived in my mailbox almost weekly, a fact of life I loved and hated. I was thrilled to be invited, for these affairs formed the backbone of our social life during seventh and eighth grades, yet what would I wear? How could I ensure that my hair be straight? Worst of all, who would dance with me?

Typically, Ben was beset by none of these questions. "Sure, I'll go," he said, as if to say "Why not?" He didn't give a thought to the fact that he didn't have a decent pair of shoes to wear, that he'd be gone from ten A.M., when services started, until four in the afternoon, that he needed to bring a present. Not surprisingly, making all the arrangements fell to me. What did you buy for a thirteen-year-old girl these days, anyway? What would be appropriate yet personal?

Oh God, I thought—would our invitations, the ones I'd carefully selected, prepared, and so recently slipped into the mail, arouse in our friends and relatives the same sense of obligation I was feeling? Would they debate whether or not to attend, worry what to wear, what to do with the kids for the day, what or how much to give?

Within a week of sending out the invitations, we received our first reply: a handwritten note accompanying the printed card we'd mailed. Now there was no turning back. I had to create lists to keep track of each response, each gift that arrived. Most people sent checks, usually with lovely notes, but some simply slipped a check into the envelope, as if to say "Here's what I owe for this event."

Why bother? I wondered as I logged these bald replies, stripped of all convention and politesse, into my filing system. In the end, we'd spend roughly as much as Ben would receive in gifts. Why not call off the party, put the money we'd earmarked for the party into Ben's account, and spare everyone the bother?

"How was the Bar Mitzvah?" I asked Ben when he returned from his first.

"Okay," he said. He had an okay time. The DJ was cool.

"Yours will be different," I told him for the hundredth time. "You'll have a lot of fun at yours."

"As long as there's a DJ and I can pick the music," he said. "As long as my friends and I can dance." Beyond that he wanted no part in the planning.

"Remind me," I said to David, "why are we doing this again?" The entire enterprise seemed suddenly absurd. One second I'd find myself contemplating the mystery of ritual, and the next deciding which drecky party favors—plastic microphones, oversize straw hats, tinny tambourines, inflatable guitars—to mail-order for our guests.

⚘

David was a leisurely, solitary shopper, and this would be the first new suit he'd purchased since our wedding, so I left him upstairs in menswear and took both boys downstairs to the junior section of Huntington's finest men's store. "We need everything," I said to the salesman, not a little embarrassed: Ben lacked not merely a suit, but an entire infrastructure—belt, socks, shoes, tie.

"Browse around," the man said. He had several other families to help, all of us in the same situation.

Ben wasted no time. Like an expert marksman stalking his prey, he narrowed his eyes and scanned the merchandise slowly, wall to wall. Then he zeroed in: "I'll take a navy blue suit, pleated pants, double-breasted jacket," he said. I hadn't even gotten my bearings—what kind of eye-smarting, consciousness-numbing gas do they pump into clothing stores, anyway?—and he'd made his decision.

On the way to the fitting room he picked up a pair of dark socks, a black belt with gold buckle, a white shirt. Then the tie. With at least fifty to choose from, he made his selection within ten seconds—an abstract but pleasing pattern in sedate blues, greens, and browns that reminded me of a Cézanne landscape.

"Done," he said triumphantly, dumping his quarry in my arms. "Can we go now?"

"You don't understand," I countered. "You have to try everything on."

"Try them on?" He looked at me as if I'd asked him to strip right there.

Our salesman finally approached, ushering Ben into the fitting room. I joined two other mothers in an anxious semi-circle. We exchanged tentative smiles: how little time had passed since we'd accompanied our sons inside. I'd even changed Ben in deserted aisles when he was a toddler. Now all we could do was wait like wallflowers.

Ben and another boy appeared at the same moment, both so mortified that neither could look at anything but his feet. "These are fine," Ben said. His shirt wasn't tucked in, the tie was draped mufflerlike around his neck, one pant leg was snagged on a sock, and his belt was unbuckled. He looked like a miniature drunk stumbling home at one A.M.

"Mom, please," he whispered in an agony of embarrassment as I moved toward him to make adjustments. Fortunately the salesman appeared, deftly knotting Ben's tie, tucking in his shirt.

Everything fit beautifully.

"What do you think?" I asked him as he turned to face the three-way mirror.

"Okay," he said. He slipped one hand into his pants pocket and touched his collar with such masculine aplomb that I wondered if he'd inhaled some kind of hormone in the fitting room. "What do *you* think?" It was the first time he'd asked my opinion all day.

"You look good," I added, something inside me telling me to keep it short and understated. Studying him, I felt older and younger at the same time—old enough to be the mother of a teenage son; young enough to remember the clammy backs of the boys I'd danced with at Bar Mitzvahs, who looked exactly as Ben did now.

"I think I'll wear it home," Ben said, shifting his weight, hooking his thumbs in his belt.

"We have to alter it," the nervous salesman said.

"He's kidding," I assured him.

Jake, too, seemed mercifully free of the shopping disability that afflicted me, blithely deciding on a navy blue sports jacket, khaki slacks, a white shirt, and bright red-and-blue tie. With his purchases under my arm, I climbed the stairs to find David rubbing the material of several suits between his thumb and forefinger. That's how my grandmother shopped. Suddenly the suburban store melted away and I was back on Division Street on the Lower East Side, where my family went to shop for good clothes. My mother needed a suit and was persuaded to try on a somber light gray skirt with a slightly flared jacket. We always went in for neutral colors, classic styles, and imperishable material. Was it possible that my grandmother, sister, and I accompanied my mother into the modest fitting room, separated from the rest of the store by a shower curtain on clattering metal hooks, while my grandfather and father kibitzed with the salesmen, dusty men, skin the color of the cartons they rested their elbows on, their hair the same color as the worn wooden floor?

David's selection wasn't classic but stylish—a light-blue-and-gray tweed that felt creamy to the touch. As he disappeared to try it on I recalled the pink madras shirt he'd purchased the day before he met my parents for the first time, his dresser drawers stuffed with nothing but ratty T-shirts. I always had a weakness for men in pink shirts. When he strolled out of the fitting room looking handsome and completely at ease, I wondered why he didn't dress up more often. But the moment he stepped onto the platform so the tailor could chalk his alterations onto the fabric, Ben came bounding over—"Hey, Dad, cool suit." And in an instant the years I'd been pushing away—all the years since the lunch when he wore the pink shirt—appeared on my husband's face and shoulders, and on his nearly bald head, and left me near tears.

In his bedroom, just after dinner, Ben took out the cassette tape of the portion of the haftarah he would read and began practicing. He played a short segment and then repeated it. He had a beautiful alto voice and an excellent ear—he'd been in the school chorus for years. He tried to match the rabbi's cantillation note for note, creating beautifully arced bits of melody, swirling away from the pitch and back to it, the way smoke rises and curls from an extinguished match. He had to learn four increasingly difficult blessings and then the segment from the haftarah itself. Practice ten minutes a day, he'd been instructed. Miraculously, he had patience for it. "I'm not used to hearing Hebrew in the house," I said to David as we cleaned the kitchen after dinner, washing and drying dishes, putting pots away, wiping down table and counter, ridding the room of the day's detritus, readying it for morning, our daily routine—comfortable, predictable, mildly tedious. But the tedium was necessary, if only to allow revelations to stand out all the more boldly. For no sooner did I put down my sponge and say, "I wish my father could hear Ben," than I realized that my father was listening to his grandson; that my son's voice encompassed the voice of every boy who ever practiced his haftarah while his parents listened, out of sight, in another room, tending to the day's exigencies.

"You need to tell me what type of music you want me to play. I'll need a song to introduce you to your guests, a song for the first dance, and one for the toast," said the DJ.

"I'll need to know which groupings of people you'll want for the formal pictures. It's best if we arrange these beforehand," said the photographer.

"Do you want the appetizer on the table when people come into the tent, or do you want it served?" asked the caterer.

"Do you want the flowers in baskets or in vases? Do you want white or yellow carnations? Do you want balloons for the children's table?" asked the florist.

I began having nightmares about the weather. Alan, the tent man, assured me that short of a typhoon we would all be safe and dry. But who wanted to be in a tent watching the rain course down the noncathedral windows?

What hallucinogenic drug was I on when I insisted that we have this party outdoors?

My mother dropped in for dinner one night, carrying a small blue box. "I wanted to give Ben Dad's tallis," she began, "but when I opened it up I saw that it was old and soiled. So I bought him a new one."

She and I climbed the stairs and knocked on his door. He was playing video games. I wished I could have prepared him; I wasn't sure how he would react. He was fully capable of shrugging it off, of barely glancing at it, saying, "Thanks," smiling falsely, and putting it down on his dresser. My mother would have been devastated—but somehow he knew that. He took it out of the box as if it were the heirloom she'd wanted it to be, and said, "Awesome." It occurred to me, with horror, that he probably didn't know what to do with it—but again he surprised me, methodically draping it over his shoulders. I knew that he thought of it as some kind of exotic cape, but to my mother his attitude seemed reverential. And he used it toward the same purpose as a religious Jew; it separated him from the world, pulled him into a kind of seclusion, altered, at least for the moment, his consciousness. "I like it," he said, as if it were part of a Halloween costume.

"This is Papa Jack's tallis case," my mother said, giving him the blue velvet envelope that I remembered my father taking with him every week to and from shul.

"One day I'll give this to my son," he said, having absorbed, on his own, without fanfare, the essence of ritual. The three of us folded the tallis, zipped it into its case, and as Ben went back to his game my mother and I looked at each other as we always did when we both found ourselves missing the same man so much that we didn't know where to begin.

"Can we select a few readings to add to the morning service in memory of family members?" I asked Rabbi Schwartz.

"Of course," he said. "Just let me know which ones you want, and then we can work them in before the Kaddish"— the traditional prayer for the dead.

Of all the tasks I had to accomplish for the Bar Mitzvah, this became paramount. I spent hours in my study, my shelves emptied of poetry books, searching for the right readings to evoke both David's sister Robbin and my father. Creating this service within a service became my passion. Sitting in solitude, lost in words, was how I'd always felt most spiritual, by which I meant most passionately involved with and yet at furthest remove from the daily nip and tuck of life.

Rocking in my rocking chair, the one I'd bought in which to nurse Ben, practicing my Hebrew, reading poems, I realized that my study had been transformed into party headquarters, ground zero of preparations, and my own private sanctuary. Every house has sacred spots. In our old apartment, it was the tiny foyer, the geographical center, from which all rooms were visible. I'd transferred that same spirit to this corner room, with its windows looking north and west. Here I felt as if I were slowly being converted to my own religion, as if Judaism were finally opening its doors to me.

A muggy Thursday evening. Ben, Jake, and I arrived at the synagogue for Ben's dress rehearsal. It was sweltering inside. Rabbi Schwartz arrived a few minutes later. He draped a tallis over Ben's Knicks shirt, placed a yarmulke on his head, and sat in a seat facing the *bimah*. "You're on, kid," he said. "Let's hear the first prayer."

Like the veteran actor he was, Ben planted his feet firmly, placed his hands on the sides of the lectern, and began praying. Nothing about him was tentative. He looked as if he'd done this all his life. He looked every inch a man.

I'd sung in enough choral concerts to know that the dress rehearsal, more than the performance, is the most gratifying moment. In front of an entire audience, on opening night, with lights in your eyes, wearing formal clothes, you scan the audience for familiar faces, worry that you'll trip or forget to come in on cue, and by the time you quell all these fears you're overcome with sadness to realize that the program is almost done and that this is the last time you'll be on this stage, singing these words. Or reading this book, climbing this mountain, or making love with this person in this way.

No, the only moment to be in the moment is during dress rehearsal. This is when you first digest the reality that after hours and hours of work you have mastered the material yet look to the world as if you learned it effortlessly, magically. The satisfaction is purely personal, dependent on no one else, the music an animal you've mounted to carry you out of time, into the distance.

This was our dress rehearsal. The climax was a hairbreadth away; I could smell it. My inner clock shifted speed. Up until a moment ago I'd been rushing toward my destination; now I wanted to slow myself down, because this was as good as it was going to get. In no time at all it would be over, and hard to recall, the way it's hard to summon the heft of a baby's bottom on your arm once he grows too heavy to lift.

Luckily I'd remembered my camera, and I took a few photos in the empty sanctuary—of Ben at the *bimah,* of his conference with the rabbi. "One day that will be you up there," I said to Jake. He looked up briefly from his math homework and nodded. "I gotta finish my work, Mom," he said.

"Perfect. Wonderful," said Rabbi Schwartz when Ben was done, walking up to the *bimah* to give him a hug, remove the tallis and yarmulke. "See you next week, when I'll hear your speech." He gave me copies of the prayers David and I would have to recite during the ceremony—in Hebrew and transliterated English.

"You'll have to help me learn this," I told Ben on the way home.

"Just take one small phrase at a time," he advised.

In my study that night, I sat in my rocking chair and tried to remember the melody Ben had just sung for me. David wandered in. "Here," I said. "We have to know these." He looked at the page, listened to my fitful starts, and said, "I know that," singing as if he were a cantor. He hadn't said these words in nearly forty years, since his own Bar Mitzvah, yet the trace memory remained. We practiced together for a few minutes, and with his help I mastered them.

"This is a first," I said as he left me to my solitude. "Singing Hebrew together." But as much as I enjoyed it, I was glad to be alone again, as if I were in my own private shul, leading a service for one.

Then I called Ellen to describe the sight of my son on the

*bimah* and how sweetly he sang. "You know," she told me, with her rare gift of saying aloud what I could never find the words to express, "your dad can hear Ben."

"I know," I said. I also knew that if my father were alive, he would be such a presence, and would exert such an influence in this process, that there would be less room for me. But I didn't say this aloud.

Memorial Day weekend our family usually went up to the Berkshires to inaugurate the summer season at my in-laws' lakefront home. But since this year the holiday preceded Ben's Bar Mitzvah by a slim week, we stayed home to tend to last minute details: final fittings, shoe polishing, and catching weather broadcasts on a nearly hourly basis.

Ben went off to a Hebrew school classmate's Bar Mitzvah at a nearby country club—the same one, coincidentally, where my senior prom, which I had boycotted, had been held. I'd graduated in 1969, when the pull of the counterculture was at its apogee, and most of my friends and I found ourselves celebrating in New York City, wandering around Greenwich Village in search of Bleecker Street.

It was also the country club at which a friend had celebrated her Sweet Sixteen, I recalled as we drove to collect

Ben late on Saturday afternoon. The Shings had played, a four-member rock band that idolized the Byrds. I had a crush on Paul, one of the guitarists. He had worn a pink oxford shirt, I remembered, the source of my fondness for shirts that color. "My God," I said to David, "I feel as if I'm reliving my entire life."

In the lobby, where we waited for our son, we listened to the cacophony of too many bands playing at once, inhaled the aroma of stale indoor air commingling with overheated food, studied the party masks that passed for faces on everyone we saw, and wondered why the place was so damn dark. Thank God, we both said to each other silently, that we stuck to our convictions, that we didn't capitulate and sign up for a place like this.

We sized up Ben's mood the moment he appeared—sullen, sulky. His arms were full of party loot—a T-shirt that read "Eric's Bar Mitzvah," personalized boxer shorts, and a host of candy and assorted *chozzerei*. We showered him with questions, which he refused to answer; in fact, he wouldn't speak to us at all until we were about five minutes from our house.

"My Bar Mitzvah is going to stink," he said. "Why couldn't we have it at that country club? It was the best."

"We went over this," I said, my heart sinking, my head throbbing. "Everyone has country club parties and they all blend into one another. Daddy and I had our wedding in a tent, and everyone remembers it, because it was so different."

"I don't want to be different," he cut me off savagely. "Why do we always have to be different? Why can't we just be like everyone else for a change? Everyone's was great and mine is going to stink. I know it. We don't have good favors, or good music or anything."

David and I couldn't look at each other. All along we'd asked Ben for his input, but he probably hadn't known enough to give informed consent until right now. And I remembered how important fitting in was at thirteen. I hadn't wanted to be different then, either. I hadn't even wanted to be Jewish.

Oh God, what if this were all a terrible miscalculation?

Thursday night, with thirty-six hours to go, I sat on the floor of my study, surrounded by mounds of candy and party favors to be divvied up among the guests. A year ago, even three months ago, I would have viewed making up goodie bags as an odious task, something to get through and finish, something ancillary to the larger effort, a waste of time and energy.

But for some reason I was enjoying myself. I enjoyed counting out pieces of candy, placing them into the plastic water bottles I'd purchased at the local discount store, and writing the name of each recipient on the side with a wide Magic Marker, making funny letters. As I wrote each child's name I thought of him or her, and also of the children who couldn't come, for whom I was also assembling a prize. The toys to be distributed at the party, the plastic, inflatable, useless things, surrounded me. Like mayflies, their life span would be measured in seconds. They were designed to self-destruct the minute they were touched. But the thought of this made me smile. They seemed symbols of largesse. Of the pleasures of the ephemeral.

Friday night, Ellen and her family arrived from Maryland; they would spend the weekend at our house. Ellen had come to help me take care of Ben the day he'd come home from the hospital. She'd sat with me as Ben wailed and told me that I wasn't a miserable failure at breast-feeding. She'd shopped for, cooked and served gourmet meals for David and me and explained, when I was on the verge of hysteria, when my life felt like something I'd wrecked in a high-speed auto chase, that crises could arise from blessed events as well as cursed ones; that I was in a crisis, that it would pass, that I'd get the hang of this motherhood thing, that we'd all be fine, that it was nonetheless all right to feel as lousy as I did.

"So tomorrow you are a man," she kidded Ben as we ate dinner together.

"You know what that means," Ellen's husband, Ron, chimed in. "You'll have to start paying your own way—chipping in for rent, buying your own clothes and food . . ."

Ben laughed and said there was nothing he'd enjoy more. He was ready to be on his own. He could handle it. All he needed was his driver's license.

After dinner Ellen and Ron stayed home with our boys so David and I could drive over to the synagogue: we had to drop off guitars and amps for the DJ and Ben and David to play tomorrow, and party favors, and the basket of yarmulkes, and the hand towels for the bathroom, and the pots of flowers I'd bought to place on the steps, and the special soaps . . . all the million and one details finally settling into place. Another caravan down Roller Coaster Road, I thought to myself. The evening felt sultry for June.

When we reached the synagogue I gasped—there it was, the blue-and-white tent, inflated like a huge balloon, obscuring the building. I walked inside. It smelled a little damp. The space seemed huge.

When I went in to say good night to Ben, I was eager to tell him how great the tent looked, how the bandstand was all set up. But he looked worried.

"I'm not really ready to be a man," he said. He found it

easier to speak to me when he wasn't looking into my eyes.

I felt like scooping him up into my arms as I had when he was a toddler. "Of course you're not," I said, stroking his hair. "No one expects you to. It's just what everyone says. You're on the road to manhood, but you're not there yet. We're not ready to let go, either. You hear me?" He said he did. And then he said he was ready for sleep.

As if it were just another workday, David and I woke up Saturday morning at five-thirty to the radio weather report. "Heavy rain," the announcer said. I ran to the window—sure enough, the clouds were thick and as steely gray as if it were January. A miserable rain was falling. "Get this," the announcer added, "possibility of hail."

David started to laugh. "Hail?" I nearly shrieked. Hail belonged in a January forecast; this was June. That's why we'd rescheduled the party in the first place. "What's next?" I said to David, envisioning a disaster of biblical proportions. "Murrain? Locusts? Boils?"

Grabbing my bathrobe, I headed for the shower—the best place to cry my eyes out.

"Don't worry," David said, waking up the boys, shoving them toward the shower. "Everything will be fine."

The drizzle persisted during our drive to the synagogue, but I forgot about the weather the moment we walked up the stairs and inside. There were two floral baskets up on the *bimah,* looking like a breath of spring; here were my mother and my sister and her family; here came the photographers, who needed to snap the posed photos before the ceremony. Then the caterer and wait staff showed up. Kitchen lights went on, the rabbi appeared and warned my father-in-law that he couldn't use his videocamera during the ceremony. But not until I saw Gloria, with her husband and daughter Sarah, Ben's oldest friend, whom I've known since she was three weeks old, when Gloria and I first got together and formed the nucleus of what would become our mothers' group, did I break into tears.

We fell into one another's arms, each of us remembering those first weeks of motherhood. How had we survived? Had anyone ever been more unprepared than we were?

By the time we filed in for services at ten o'clock the room was brimming with people. "Who cares about the weather?" Jake asked with characteristic wisdom as the rabbi intoned the first of the morning's prayers. He's right, I thought, watching Ben make his way to the *bimah* to join the rabbi. Nothing could ruin this. Certainly nothing as trivial as weather. Only then did I notice through the twelve windows overlooking the wooded hillside that the sky had indeed lightened.

My mother put the tallis around Ben, who gave his

speech with true aplomb and presence, milking the laughs, announcing that he would continue his Hebrew studies next year at Senior Seminar. Jake spoke; I read my speech, David ad-libbed his.

Torahs were removed from the ark, lifted up, read, lifted up, marched around the room, replaced. David and I sang our prayers, Ben chanted the prayers and his portion, the people we selected for honors were called to the Torah.

Just before the close of services, when Kaddish was usually read, David and I came to the *bimah* one more time to read the poems for our sister and father. "The last conversation I had with my father," I said by way of introduction, "was about Ben's Bar Mitzvah. He so wanted to be here. And I know he is. This poem, an excerpt from Theodore Roethke's 'The Far Field,' is in his memory."

> *I learned not to fear infinity,*
> *The far field, the windy cliffs of forever,*
> *The dying of time in the white light of tomorrow,*
> *The wheel turning away from itself,*
> *The sprawl of the wave,*
> *The on-coming water . . .*
>
> *All finite things reveal infinitude:*
> *The mountain with its singular bright shade*
> *Like the blue shine on freshly frozen snow,*

The after-light upon ice-burdened pines;
Odor of basswood on a mountain-slope,
A scent beloved of bees;
Silence of water above a sunken tree:
The pure serene of memory in one man,—
A ripple widening from a single stone
Winding around the waters of the world.

For Robbin, David read May Sarton's "Song."

Now let us honor with violin and flute
A woman set so deeply in devotion
That three times blasted to the root
Still she grew green and poured strength out.

Still she stood fair, providing the cool shade,
Compassion, the thousand leaves of mercy,
The cherishing green hope. Still like a tree she stood,
Clear comfort in the town and all the neighborhood.

Pure as the tree is pure, young
As the tree forever young, magnanimous
And natural, sweetly serving: for her the song,
For her the flute sound and the violin be strung.

For her all love, all praise,
All honor, as for trees
In the hot summer days.

I looked out to our friends and family as David read. In the midst of happiness, sadness. In the midst of plenty, absence. In the midst of life, death. These were no longer opposites; they were the same single thing. The readings were working their magic: people sat up, listened, were moved. Some cried. I felt beyond tears, closer to whatever resided on the other side.

The service closed with the singing of "Adon Olom," one of the first songs my grandmother taught me on the toy piano. Everyone's here, I thought to myself, the room bulging with guests, invited and un-, alive and dead, everyone I ever cared about present, as if time itself had become unhinged.

Three hours later it was all over. It was hot and steamy under the tent, but we were surrounded by hazy sunshine. Dancing, singing, eating swirled around me, but I walked through the afternoon as dazed as I had at my wedding, unable to eat or drink, wanting simply to talk with everyone, to thank them for coming, to tell them I loved them.

I remember Ben at the microphone calling up people to light a candle on his guitar-shaped cake with him, a task usually left to the emcee, but which he gladly usurped. He and his friend joined the DJ at the bandstand and played electric guitar; David sat in for a song or two. The happiest photo of David I have is taken at that moment.

My friend Pam said, "I heard a rumor that you're wearing your wedding dress."

My college friend Nancy, who'd been at my wedding, said, "It's like a time warp to have Ellen and everyone here, as if no time has passed at all."

Our friend Bob, who would celebrate his son's Bar Mitzvah in six more years, said, "You guys are my heroes. You managed to pull off an affair like this in a way that's totally real. It's entirely your family. Nothing fake or phony about it."

Our friend Jordan, who would celebrate his son's Bar Mitzvah in a year, said, "I feel as if this event defines us as adults."

My great-aunt Marion said, "I remember Ben's *brith*. Soon you'll dance at his wedding."

Ben said, "This was the best Bar Mitzvah I've ever been to. The best. Even my friends loved it."

By four nearly everyone had left. Ben and his dad packed their musical equipment; I distributed the checks to the caterer, the DJ, the waiters, the custodian. I thanked everyone for coming.

And then we drove home.

"You must be exhausted."

"You must need a vacation."

"You must be feeling let-down."

"You must feel as if it never happened."

None of those was true. It was odd, driving to Hebrew school on Tuesday and seeing an empty yard where the tent once stood. "Brigadoon," I said aloud, a reference neither of my sons understood.

I had braced myself for an onslaught of postpartum blues, but they never arrived. Uncharacteristically, I was calm, relaxed, serene. Grateful that we'd been able to host such a party, that we'd pulled it off, that most people understood what we were offering and appreciated it. Eager to get back to work. Regretless, except that we couldn't have invited more people. Relieved that I no longer had to worry about the weather. Eager to describe what I'd just undergone.

Abraham Joshua Heschel, I'd read, described the Sabbath ritual as "a palace in time." But to me, ritual felt more like a shack, a modest dwelling you hammer together yourself out of planks you find lying about and bent nails—like the *succah,* the little booth in which religious Jews eat during the harvest holiday, built each fall and then disassembled only to be reconstructed next year. A place where you can stop resisting those raucous, graceless contradictory feelings we keep at bay so much of the time. A place in which you can open the window a crack and let them in, watch them run riot like dogs too long cooped up, get the better of us, parade before us in all their shameless vanity and urgency, taunting our feeble efforts to tame them. For we can never master paradox. We can only address it the way a frantic mother does her wayward child who shows up hours late: "Do you have any idea how worried I was about you?" because she's mad and sad and relieved and scared all at once. You can only sit with it, the way you endure your enemy on those occasions when you find yourselves in the same room, breathing the same air, forced to admire, if only grudgingly, each other's good looks.

Ritual, I realize, resuming my work, is all of these: a place and a time, a journey and a stopover, a process through which we absorb paradox, transcend time and place, past and future, male and female, certainty and uncertainty, inclusion and exclusion—all experience that defies explanation.

A card addressed to Ben arrived a few days later from a good friend of mine. "Happy journey," he wrote.

C H A P T E R   6

*Worldly/Holy*

hristmas Eve 1968. I'm alone in the living room—everyone else has long since gone to bed—reading Kazantzakis's *The Last Temptation of Christ*. I've been portioning out the chapters so that I can finish it as close to the stroke of midnight as possible.

After turning the last page, I hold the book for a while, unwilling to let it out of my grasp. I think of my friend Ellen, who is at this moment in Bethlehem with her family. She is the luckiest person I know.

"Silent night," I begin to sing to myself, thinking of the pilgrims kneeling in churches around the world for midnight mass, for whom the mysteries of the virgin birth and Immaculate Conception make sense, cutting below rational understanding, releasing them from the need to understand miracles through logical means.

I remember standing at my apartment window, looking at Christian girls dressed up as brides for their confirmation. If anything, my love for Christianity, with its promise of all-embracing love, the triumph of mercy over justice, of redemption—has deepened over the years. Sometimes I think about becoming a nun, sequestering myself from the world, losing myself in continuous prayer.

Hanukkah's a wisp of a holiday, I think, walking into the dining room where our menorah sits on a tray in a waxen puddle. Christmas is like a relative who moves in, or like a piano, something with weight and heft, which takes up position in a place of prominence—the corner by the window, the head of the table—and draws everyone to it. Showy and splashy, it glimmers and shines and twinkles; it's a big birthday party, with cake and presents for everyone. The stern, harsh, demanding God of Moses celebrates no birthday or anniversary, with pure, unalloyed major-key joy. "Never forget." "Always remember." These injunctions to keep the immense oceanic sadness of the past alive are embedded in the very heart of Judaism. Every Jewish holiday has an edge of sadness, even the holidays of liberation such as Purim, Passover, and Hanukkah. There's a darkness to them, a sense of victory wrested from the jaws of defeat, of impending heartbreak the moment you give in to repose.

There are no songs like "Adeste Fidelis," which I begin to sing next, the Latin satisfyingly clean, enunciated in the front of the mouth, involving the tip of the tongue and teeth. I know all the carols; I've memorized them. They're everywhere—on television and in stores. But I also learn them in school, in chorus, during our rehearsals for winter concerts, which are really Christmas concerts, since most of the songs we sing are carols. The repertoire is always leavened, of course, with a few Hanukkah songs—strange Hebrew words, syncopated tempos, minor melodies that never crescendo or soar at the end but simply peter out, like extinguished candles. I hate them. Everyone does—only we aren't allowed to say so. They are an interlude, something to get through until launching into "Hark the Herald Angels Sing," or "O Tannenbaum." Even the haunting "God Rest Ye Merry, Gentlemen," with its minor cast, has an uplift to it, while every Jewish song, no matter how joyous, is built on sadness, on loss. Who wouldn't prefer the blare of trumpets proclaiming, as Kazantzakis did, "It is accomplished!"—the ascension to another world, a miraculous world, where every ending is happy, every injustice redressed.

December 1994. What a familiar sensation, to be wearing a white blouse and long black skirt and standing shoulder to slightly sweaty shoulder on auditorium risers. The community chorus I joined was performing the Mozart "Requiem." The prospect of singing this piece was what originally propelled me to join the chorus; I'd sung it years ago, in St. Paul's, a circular jewel of a church on the Columbia University campus, where our collegiate voices filled the holy space and sounded as close to angelic as I'd ever experienced.

In the Northport High School auditorium, our voices sounded less celestial, but we were well rehearsed and sang our hearts out. The interplay among chorus, conductor, and soloists was airtight. It was a punishing piece, demanding musically and emotionally, even for me, and I am one of the younger members of the choir. In college we carried nothing in our music folders but the music; now we all packed tissues, cough drops, and bifocals and helped steady one another under the glare of the lights.

During intermission we wiped our brows, cleaned our glasses, sucked our lozenges. I was exhausted and wanted nothing more than to greet my husband and loyal fans in the audience, receive their kudos, and head home.

But we had a second half of the program to perform—"holiday" songs, which meant eight Christmas carols and one Hanukkah song, a schmaltzy, sanitized version of a Hebrew melody that swelled like a Broadway show tune on the word "freedom." The front of the stage was lined with poinsettias;

how did I not notice this during the "Requiem"? Concealed in our black music folders were tiny flashlights in the shape of candles: when it was time for "Silent Night," our last number, our conductor would give us the signal to turn them on. We would hold them up in front of our music as the house lights gradually dimmed. By the song's end, only the candle lights would be visible in the darkness—the climax of the performance.

This was precisely the kind of moment I'd imagined staging for myself when I sat in my parents' living room as a teenager, with Kazantzakis on my lap. But now, on the risers, in the middle of "O Come All Ye Faithful," I felt unusually uncomfortable, agitated. Something was askew. I felt on my face the same kind of scowl you get from eating something that's slightly off. I was recoiling from the music, singing it against my better judgment. Suddenly I wanted to be anywhere but here. My queasiness intensified when we came to the Hanukkah song—this pathetic offering that was supposed to balance the program, to defuse anyone's objection—as if thirty-two measures of music in a language no one understood, in a key no one could whistle, would counterbalance the weight of all those carols, of hundreds of years of Christmas music.

On my face was an expression I knew well, having seen it on my parents' faces after each concert of mine they'd dutifully attended, from junior high through graduate school. They couldn't not come if I were performing—they were too loyal to boycott—but it pained them, and their pain infuriated me. How small-minded, how petty, to become snared on the words and ignore the music. Glorifying God was glorifying God, no matter what the language. Couldn't they transcend the superficial differences and penetrate to the heart of the mystery?

Yet here I stood, knee-deep into "It Came upon a Midnight Clear," feeling exactly as they had. This music no longer spoke to me; and when it did speak, it whispered of oppression, of hegemony. It was airless music; it allowed no room for other scales, other ways of worship. It blared on and on, as if the entire world were Christian.

I can't do this, I said to myself. I wouldn't disturb the performance—I'd finish singing "Silent Night," I'd light my candle—but I wouldn't do it again. Standing there in the dark, as holy silence descended on the auditorium, I could sense all the people around me summoning their most meaningful, most touching memories and recollections of Christmas. A lovely tableau, but one without a place for me.

And then I was hit with a realization that nearly knocked me off the risers: My love for Christianity was rooted in self-hate, and always had been. For years I'd maintained that I'd never experienced any prejudice—no one had ever called me a kike or dirty Jew, no door had ever been closed to me because of my religion; if anything, I felt more discrimination as a woman. So I'd blithely assumed that I'd never been targeted, only to realize, now, that anti-Semitism had entered my awareness without my knowing it. I'd absorbed millennia of suspicion and hatred so stealthily that it didn't register on my consciousness but went directly to my fantasies, where I'd hammered it into a desire to be what I wasn't. I didn't want to be different; I wanted to move in concert with the world, without friction.

No more. The music no longer moved me, and friction no longer scared me. I felt as if I'd been in self-imposed exile, and now it was time to come home.

September 1995. Though I was starting only my second year on the board of trustees of the synagogue, I felt like a veteran. An always surprising mix of business, theology, and philosophy, the meetings were a study in group process and a crash course for me in organizational studies. The lesson I had to learn anew each time was how much advance work and planning even the smallest endeavor—a yard sale, a policy statement—required.

The synagogue was becoming a contained world in

miniature, the way high school had been. Feeding on familiarity, needing to bank on the fact that we shared certain basic assumptions, I grew increasingly comfortable and more
willing to volunteer, to try on various positions until I found
one or two that fit well. There was no shortage of good causes
needing attention. I volunteered to serve as the liaison to the
regional Reconstructionist council in Manhattan, and as a
member of the Social Action and Development Committees.
I also became chair of the committee to welcome homosex-
ual Jews. And, of course, I was still taking minutes at every
board meeting.

Should we start a search for a new cantor for next year's
High Holy Day services? Or should we recognize the fact that
we needed a full-time cantor, to lead services, teach in the
Hebrew school? Everyone had an opinion that differed
slightly from her neighbor's. In the midst of this debate,
someone mused, "Maybe we can't afford a cantor yet, but
wouldn't it be great if we had our own chorus?"

"We used to, years ago," said Carol. "We kept it going for
about three years. You need a conductor, though."

"Well, I have choral experience," volunteered Steve, the
treasurer. "I could probably lead it."

After countless consultations, phone calls, and rough
drafts, Carol and I sent out a flyer asking for singers to join
us, and twelve of us showed up at Carol's house one Tuesday

evening. Together we plowed through the formidable stack of sheet music she'd accumulated over the years and selected four songs, our goal to prepare a short program to sing during Rosh Hashanah services, barely a month away.

Our first selection was "By the Waters of Babylon," a plaintive four-part round. I plunked out the melody on the piano as Steve conducted. It was slow going. Although we had several accomplished musicians among us, some knew music only by ear and couldn't read notes, and a few others had difficulty finding and staying on pitch.

What did I get myself into? I wondered, dispiritedly hammering out the same basic melody on the piano time after time. Any choral group for which I was the accompanist was in sad shape—I was a much more competent singer than pianist. What had possessed me to drop out of a chorus in which I was among the least capable, which I was allowed to join because I so fervently asked to be included after stinking up my audition, where we mastered eight-part harmony without breaking a sweat?

But I knew the answer. Marking time at the piano, I slowly realized that in the absence of a musical challenge I was face-to-face with another one. This particular chorus wasn't about musical sophistication or perfection. It wasn't about sounding angelic. What rescued these homespun rehearsals from musical oblivion was the pleasure of coming together, of being together, of performing together for our families, our congregation. As we sang "Osey Shalom," I knew each of us was summoning memories that paralleled mine, of my time-traveling grandmother who lit candles in the near dark of a Sabbath evening and taught me the wordless melodies she'd learned in another country, from a mother of whom not even a photo survives, in a community now all but obliterated. We were tapping into one of Judaism's deepest wellsprings when we sang.

How we congratulated each other when we'd learned the songs. "Wait a second," Carol said, interrupting our jubilation. "We still have lots of work to do."

We looked at her, dumbstruck. Whatever could she mean? Apparently we'd overlooked the fact that in this operation, the singers weren't simply performers, but also producers, stage hands, publicity agents, and choreographers. We had to decide how to dress (any way we liked), how to sit (with our families, not as a group), how to hold our music (in black folders, which had to be purchased and distributed), how to line up (first sopranos, then altos), where to stand, how to walk off. Even the tiniest decision, it seemed, spawned more decisions than I could have imagined. For all my past choral experience, I'd never had to think for a moment about any of these details. I'd simply shown up.

Just as I had at my wedding, and my sons' *briths*. As I had wanted to do at Ben's Bar Mitzvah. But apparently that way of worship, of observance, was no longer an option for me. There was no sidestepping the issue of engagement. "According to the toil," says the Talmud, "the reward."

"Not only do we have to go to services," I announced to my family a few days before Rosh Hashanah, "but we have to be there early, nine-fifteen, so Dad can set up his equipment"— David having generously consented to accompany the chorus on electric guitar. Instead of complaining, as I thought they might, my sons were tantalized, delighted by the fact that they were somehow included, if only as schleppers of amps and microphones.

When we arrived at the church, we had our pick of parking spaces. The still-empty gym with row after row of aligned folding chairs looked eerily cavernous. Only a handful of members had arrived before us—the head of the Ritual Committee moving the portable ark containing the Torahs to center stage, members of the committee stacking prayer books, the rabbi adjusting his microphone, the president of the congregation going over her speech. How much scaffolding goes into these events, I realized yet again, how much behind-the-scenes preparation to mount the spectacle of a worship service. Nothing comes automatically or without personal sacrifice; nowhere is the boundary between the secular and the spiritual more blurred.

As other chorus members began arriving, we decided to warm up. Steve found a side door that opened onto a courtyard; like a heavenly choir, we gathered outside, opened our music, and began running through our songs. Thanks to the echo, we sounded twice our size, our voices carrying out into the street, greeting all who came.

Within fifteen minutes of the start of services, we were on stage, performing. We couldn't stand quite the way we'd intended, and it was difficult for us to hear David's guitar over the buzz of conversation. Were our voices carrying to the back of the room? Why weren't Ben and Jake in their seats, instead of sitting near their father, on stage, looking as if they had important jobs to do, their shirts already untucked? And then our program was over. To enthusiastic applause, we walked off the stage and back to our waiting families.

Oddly, neither Ben nor Jake seemed in a hurry to leave. The attention they received, as roadies, seemed to compensate for the droning on of the service. They sat, for a change, and asked questions. To me, the morning seemed transformed: the boys less restive, the pace brisker, the prayers more plangent. I shouldn't have been so surprised; it was the lesson of the Bar Mitzvah all over again—finding a way to contribute to, to participate in, a service imbues it with new meaning. Personal significance does not reside within and cannot be extracted from ritual simply by standing up and sitting down, by reading this prayer or that one. We can't show up empty-handed like an inconsiderate guest, but must come with an offering; we each have to sculpt our own service from the larger block of what goes on at the ark, on the *bimah*. And then you sit back and see what happens.

This year, when the ram's horn was blown, I felt like crying. It resonated within me in a way it never had. I reached out to touch everyone in my family, to hold them close, and found myself spontaneously praying for our health and safety in the coming year. "*L'shana tovah,*" is what everyone says to each other—which means "Happy New Year" in Hebrew, an open-voweled, sweet-sounding language. "*A guten yahr,*" I said mostly to myself but slightly aloud, hearing my grandmother's guttural Yiddish, "*alevi.*"

"Have you noticed how much more Yiddish is sneaking into your conversation?" my friend Ellen had asked me recently . Actually I hadn't, but of course she was right. I routinely tossed off *shul, haimish,* and *freilich,* as in, "Our chorus isn't very accomplished, but when we get together it's very *freilich.*" These words nailed my feelings, Yiddish oddly comfortable and resonant. It was the closest I came to being bilingual. Most remarkable of all, I couldn't remember what I'd ever held against it. That it had once revolted me was a historical fact, but nothing I could summon up. I used it as punctuation when I was moved to; if anything, I delighted in injecting it into certain conversations. It was a way of letting down my hair, of being intimate, while at the same time standing slightly apart.

Ben followed through on his decision to attend Senior Seminar, a post–Bar Mitzvah class that met each Sunday with the rabbi. "I took a class like this after my Bar Mitzvah," the rabbi explained, "during which my teacher told us about the civil rights movement, the antiwar movement . . ." This course similarly intertwined religious studies and current events, with the goal of introducing young adults to the Jewish commandment of *tikkun olam,* or repair of the world. Ben took a seat at the head of the table, opposite the rabbi, thoroughly engaged.

Jacob began Hebrew school. We commenced another round of afternoon drives down Roller Coaster Road and of answering why it's essential to go to Hebrew school. My thoughts sometimes strayed to his Bar Mitzvah, where we'd have it, how we'd make it special.

The first Tuesday of the month—time for a board meeting. I packed my compendium of minutes, bade my family good night, and picked up Vicki. Our lives were on such parallel tracks, in terms of career, children, and marriage, that we had too much to talk about any single time we met. But at least half of every conversation was taken up with synagogue news or gossip.

Many potentially divisive issues had arisen in the past few months. Slowly, with reluctance, I came to recognize that the board, and the congregation at large, wasn't as homogeneous as I'd assumed, that substantive differences divided us on lofty as well as quotidian issues. Should we launch a capital campaign to raise money to pay off the mortgage? Should we adopt a policy that officially and overtly welcomed gay and lesbian Jews into our congregation? Should we give special recognition to the person who donated a stained-glass window rescued from a Brooklyn shul, or would this contradict our long-standing egalitarian policy?

Politics, whether on the federal, local, or religious level, rarely transcends the kind of bickering, ad hominem attacks, retribution seeking, and back stabbing that erupts in eighth-grade lunchrooms. Factions emerge; alliances form, shift, and re-form; people aggrandize and abase themselves; pettiness does battle with high-mindedness. After two years of not having opinions, not only was I suddenly full of them, but I found myself ready to take on the thorniest problems. Even more surprising, I gravitated toward unpopular, minority positions, where I found myself in the company of older members, including many original members.

Kehillath Shalom had been founded as a protest, the result of a schism. In 1969, with anti–Vietnam War fervor cresting, the rabbi at a Conservative synagogue in Huntington, whose sermons were becoming increasingly political, envisioned a program whereby speakers would be invited into the synagogue to debate the issues of the day. His contract was not renewed. A handful of congregants—ten or twelve like-minded families, who believed with the rabbi that Judaism was not a bloated ark floating above the waters of current events, but a lighter, lither vessel, more like a kayak that thrust you into the belly of the roiling waters—resigned and formed their own congregation. Until a wealthy heiress donated her home on Goose Hill Road to the fledgling congregation, rabbi and followers met in an American Legion Hall and then at a church. By the time they began carving a synagogue out of living and dining rooms, fifty families had joined. Their first Rosh Hashanah service was celebrated in September 1969—the year I went to college—at St. Patrick's Church in Huntington. The new synagogue was committed to equality, egalitarianism—no sisterhood and men's club, no building fund ("We didn't want to develop an edifice complex," one of the founding members explained to me)—and political activism. They vowed that their membership would not exceed ninety families.

We still had no sisterhood or men's club, and we still had a commitment to treating all members equally—no plaques on walls announcing generous donations—but we did have a building fund. Our membership totaled nearly two hundred families—and we were greedy for more. In fact, one of the reasons the board voted to take out a mortgage to renovate and expand the original building was to attract new members. But none of the new leadership had stopped to consider how quality changes as quantity does. And some of us began to wonder if the people we were attracting cared more for the edifice than what was within.

Maybe it was time for a new synagogue to calve itself, the way Kehillath Shalom had. Maybe there's a critical mass beyond which heterogeneity works against principles. I was certainly feeling the strain. Looking around the table at board meetings, I saw a contingent of businesspeople whose pragmatic approach to the issues on the table was often at odds with mine. Debates were tinged with acrimony. I found myself sounding dangerously self-righteous, spouting aphorisms like "What good is it if we fill our coffers but lose our soul?"

Vicki and I, philosophical comrades, left these meetings literally quaking. During the car ride home we replayed each exchange, savoring each revealing comment, lauding those who gave eloquence to our point of view, deploring those who sought to exploit a division between the older and newer members. We, oddly enough, found ourselves siding with the former; though twenty years separated us, we shared a heartening idealism, a sense that a synagogue was more than a business and had to keep its eye on more than the bottom line.

Maybe I was too idealistic, I thought after dropping Vicki off at her house and driving the few blocks home. Maybe I had romanticized the synagogue, assumed that our similarities outweighed our differences. Maybe it wasn't as much of a sanctuary as I wished it to be. This was the same dilemma faced by Jews of every age, since they were a small tribe wandering in the desert—how to maintain spirituality in an overwhelmingly secular world. How to maintain group ethos in the face of encroaching individuality. Three Jews, four opinions.

Though the politics of the board were wrenching, music calmed me. We met weekly, either at the synagogue or Carol's house, to rehearse the Hanukkah program we'd put together—two liturgical songs to perform during the Friday night service, "Hatikvah," the Israeli national anthem, and three rousing holiday songs, including a rendition of Peter, Paul, and Mary's "Light One Candle."

*Hatikvah,* which means "hope," was a demanding song to learn—rhythm changes in each verse, dramatic dynamic variation, and a mouthful of words to enunciate. We spent hours struggling with the music, wrestling with it, as if we were Jacob and his angel. Countless evenings I lost patience, sitting at the keyboard, trying to sing and plunk out notes, trying to remember all the pointers I'd heard from all the choral directors I'd worked with over the years. Once, the amateurishness and hopelessness of our endeavor moved me to frustrated tears.

One night only six of us showed up, and rather than cancel the rehearsal, we decided to go through the music together. We stood in the center of Carol's beautiful living room, the group's strongest singers, the ones with the most musical training, and what we heard astonished us. I knew we were all thinking the same thought: Why not recompose the chorus—kick out those who didn't show up, those who couldn't read music or stay on pitch—and sing ourselves? What was preventing us?

Love stopped us—love alone. Love for our absent choir members and for the idea of community, of an embracing, welcoming sister- and brotherhood that held out its arms to anyone and everyone who wanted to join, who wanted to lift up her voice, or donate a stained-glass window, or light a memorial candle, or offer a prayer. Yes, come stand with us. Let's choose to be together.

The Friday night of our performance, as I took my seat in the front of the sanctuary, I realized that this was the first time I'd ever been to a regular service in the shul. I'd shown up for Bar Mitzvahs, synagogue dedications, New Year's services—the big-ticket items of worship. This familiar rising up and facing the door to welcome the Sabbath bride, this lighting of candles, went on every Friday, without fanfare, the bread-and-butter of Jewish observance. Because the Torah is not taken from the ark on Friday nights, the service had no climax. It just ambled along, unhurriedly. Studying the faces around me, I felt as if I were in the midst of a family gathering, in an uncluttered living room that just happened to have a soaring cedar ceiling. Most surprisingly, I was able to take in the rabbi's words—about the miracle of Hanukkah, about the even more miraculous miracle of the Sabbath, the Jews'

major contribution to religion after monotheism. Even the prayers didn't bounce off me, as if I were wearing a shield, but penetrated. I hadn't been feeling particularly peaceful when I entered the synagogue, but moment by moment peacefulness seeped in, and I felt as if I'd taken a vacation from myself, from everyday life, into the realm of Shabbat.

In the past I'd rebelled against the very notion of Shabbat, of scheduling times for rest or spirituality. My desire or need to feel spiritual waxed and waned according to no timetable or calendar. Yet something had happened to me over the course of the service. Restfulness had worked its way into my consciousness, from the outside in. Maybe I shouldn't have been so surprised. As a writer, I knew better than to wait for inspiration; I showed up at my keyboard every morning whether I felt like it or not. And sometimes those days that began with the least promise—because I had a headache, or a fight with my son, or an unpleasant conversation with an editor—ended up proving the most constructive. You never knew. Apparently it never hurt to show up and see what happened.

Our voices, when we stood to perform, took on an entirely different timbre in the much smaller sanctuary than they had in the expansive church gym. "Smile," Carol pantomimed to us as we stood in an earnest group around the lectern in the center of the *bimah,* our eyes glued to Steve for our cues. "Light One Candle" brought the congregation to its feet, the last chord resonating in the sanctuary for what felt like minutes.

"It was a good concert," David said on the ride home. His driving guitar had urged us on during the Peter, Paul, and Mary song, pushing us to new intensity. I was thinking thoughts less about the performance, though, than about an incident during a recent rehearsal.

During a short break, we were trying to plan ahead for our next Rosh Hashanah service, casting about for a new song to add to our repertoire. "You know what I love, and would love to see us perform?" mused Steve. "Alvenu Malkenu."

Yes, we all nodded and smiled; it was a beautiful song. Then from the silence, without looking at anybody else, we all began singing it, first to ourselves, gradually louder, then at concert level. No music, no leader, not even looking at each other—most of us had our eyes closed, reliving our own most private memories—we sang the haunting lines in perfect synchrony. And then, in concert still, we came to the end of the song, our voices diminished, fading into silence.

"I have a crazy proposition for you," I said to Vicki five o'clock one Friday afternoon. "There's a contemplative Shabbat service tonight at eight o'clock. I'm thinking of going. Want to come?"

"Sure," she said, sounding more eager than I'd anticipated.

"Do you realize," I asked, driving with her along the familiar roads, "that this is the first time, of all our times going to synagogue together, that we're going for a service and not a meeting?"

If religion were a house, then Vicki and I had found our way in through the basement or a side door. We were servants, caretakers, who showed up to keep the place running, incredulous to find ourselves inside by any entrance. Tonight, though, we'd go in through the front door, through worship, a desire to pray.

"Are you sure it's tonight?" Vicki asked as we approached the synagogue. Only three or four cars were in the parking lot. But a sign—"Contemplative Shabbat service in progress"—was posted on the synagogue door. "Please enter in silence." The chairs in the sanctuary were drawn into a circle. Eight people were gathered, their eyes closed, some on the floor, some on cushions or prayer benches, some simply in their seats. The lights were dim; even the Eternal Flame seemed to burn at a slightly lower wattage. Vicki and I took seats next to each other and closed our eyes.

Only recently had I become aware that Judaism had its own meditative tradition, paralleling the monastic Christian orders and Eastern religions. Though it had never been incorporated into mainstream, rabbinic Judaism, which stressed biblical and talmudic exegesis, it nonetheless survived through the centuries. Now Evelyn Botkin, a woman in our congregation, had taken it upon herself to create a special service out of this tradition—she'd composed a prayer book and begun holding contemplative Shabbat services. I'd been planning to attend for months, but it seemed as if the more I needed an excuse to meditate, the harder it was to extricate myself from my life and attend.

I'd dabbled in meditation for years, reading about it, asking people about how they did it, trying my own patchwork version of it for one or two days in a row before abandoning it. Most of what I knew came from my Lamaze class when I was pregnant with Ben; in fact, it was the voice of my Lamaze teacher, Elizabeth Bing, which I heard now, coaxing me to "take a cleansing breath, in through your nose, out through your mouth."

As her voice rang in my ear, I realized it was actually juxtaposed with another's, with the man who taught at the studio where, for a year or so, I'd studied yoga. As physical types, they couldn't have been more polar opposites: he was black, young, tall, supple, bald, muscular, deep voiced; she white, old, white haired, hunched over, feathery, her voice breaking with age as I remember my grandmother's had. As a yoga student I'd been young and muscular, stretched out on a thin blue mat or sitting with my spine straight, legs crossed, palms upturned, breathing deeply, watching my thoughts float by me as if on an endless, churning river. Eight months pregnant, I'd leaned against a pillow and David, feeling like a beached whale, hand draped over my huge belly, trying to commune with my unborn child.

Yet during this quiet time in the sanctuary both teachers' voices blended into one; both versions of my former self merged into my present body as I tried to let my thoughts go, as I tried to concentrate on breathing in and breathing out, in and out. "Focus on a part of your body," suggested Evelyn, who had led each contemplative service, "your nostrils, or your lungs, or your diaphragm. Label those thoughts that snag you—'That's a worried thought,' or 'That's a planning thought' " Her suggestions were very helpful. I found myself settling toward some sense of inner bottom. My pulse faded into a quieter rhythm. I envisioned my breath entering my head, gushing upward through the Augean stables of my brain like a roiling, flood-swollen river and exiting, a thin, clear stream.

"Open your eyes when you're ready," Evelyn said. It was a surprisingly easy reentry—no jarring lights, no sounds save for the companionable ticking of an invisible clock. She asked us to read from the prayer book she had compiled, to stand to welcome the Sabbath bride. This was a Friday night service stripped of all but its essentials, with long periods of meditation cushioning each of the traditional prayers.

When I sensed the service drawing to a close, I looked at my watch, thinking that an hour had passed. But it was nearly ten o'clock.

"Pure prayer begins at the threshold of silence," writes Stephen Mitchell in *The Book of Psalms.* "It says nothing, asks for nothing. It is a kind of listening. The deeper the listening, the less we listen for, until the silence itself becomes the voice of God."

I memorized this quote during the service and turned it over in my mind for several days. I believe in its wisdom: only when we stop listening for something are we free to truly hear.

But if the time I'd devoted to the synagogue has taught me anything, it's that there are many types of prayer, many ways of believing. Judaism, perhaps all religions, flourishes where tension is highest—on the tenuous ground between the here and now and forever, the secular and the holy, the feminine and the masculine, the group and individual, self and other, spontaneity and rote. Like a desert flower, one with shallow but tenacious roots, it seeks out the most improbable, inhospitable crevices and fault lines in which to grow. Like a toddler, it's inexplicably and incessantly drawn to danger: the flame, the precipice. It's an unwieldy patchwork, an impossible amalgam, an uneasy peace that needs constant rejiggering, an insistent voice in your ear that won't stop suggesting that maybe, just maybe, there's more here than meets the eye.

"What happens after you die, Mom?" Jacob, now nine, scares himself before sleep with thoughts of eternity. I wonder if he's thinking of the big Ferris wheel, as I did. But before I can answer, he answers himself.

"I think we are born again. I think there are seven stages to life, and death is only a stage. Then we come back. . . ." He spins his cosmology to me, and I wonder from where he derived it. My Hindu son.

"Do you believe in God?" he asks me.

Ah. Finally. The question I've been waiting for. The one I thought the rabbi was poised to ask. The one that had to be answered before anything else.

"Yes," I said. "In a way. I don't believe in a God in the sky."

"I don't either," he said quickly.

"But I believe that God is inside us. God is like our breath—we can't see it, but it fills us, and urges us to live."

"I wish I knew Papa Jack," he says. I can follow his association: I always tell him that his grandfather's spirit is alive inside him.

"I do too," I tell him. What delight my father would take in this child, his grandson. What tactile pleasure. Until his final illness, my father never outgrew his boyish capacity to experience pleasure in his whole body. His happiness overflowed his hands, his eyes.

"I hope we all get to see each other after we're dead," Jake tells me, his small body almost shaking in earnestness.

"I do too," I tell him, hoping he won't ask me if I believe as he does, for my answer is constantly changing. Sometimes it seems an extravagance to believe in a spiritual hereafter, in the sense that everything spiritual is a luxury, a superfluity—not essential in the way that food, water, and shelter are.

Honestly, I remain an agnostic. But I want Jake to be right. Wanting has to count for something; it's no more insubstantial than believing.

I'm walking with Carol on the boardwalk at Sunken Meadow Beach, a few miles from my house. Our conversation always moves in unexpected directions, associatively, using dream logic. She begins to talk about the early days of the shul, why she joined, how she came to become president. She says that every institution has to evolve, or it dies. She asks me what the synagogue means to me.

I remember Eve Lodge's voice on the phone, her patience, her optimism that I'd find a way to participate. "I need the shul for a lot of reasons," I tell her. "It's a way for me to feel part of a community, to do good work, to pass along tradition to my sons. Sometimes I think that for me it's about everything but God."

"What if everything's God?" she asks.

What if.

Dear Grandma, you gave me the music, but the words you mumbled were wrong. The religion you bequeathed me isn't about what can't be, what shouldn't be done. It's about possibility.

Printed in the United States
By Bookmasters